KU-571-609

Essential Histories

The Hundred Years' War

1337-1453

Anne Curry

OSPREY
PUBLISHING

First published in Great Britain in 2002 by Osprey Publishing,
Elms Court, Chapel Way, Botley, Oxford OX2 9LP, UK.
Email: info@ospreypublishing.com

© 2002 Osprey Publishing Limited

All rights reserved. Apart from any fair dealing for the purpose
of private study, research, criticism or review, as permitted under
the Copyright, Design and Patents Act, 1988, no part of this
publication may be reproduced, stored in a retrieval system, or
transmitted in any form or by any means, electronic, electrical,
chemical, mechanical, optical, photocopying, recording or
otherwise, without the prior written permission of the copyright
owner. Enquiries should be made to the Publishers.

Every attempt has been made by the publisher to secure the
appropriate permissions for material reproduced in this book. If
there has been any oversight we will be happy to rectify the
situation and written submission should be made to the
Publishers.

ISBN 1 84176 269 5

Editor: Rebecca Cullen
Design: Ken Vail Graphic Design, Cambridge, UK
Cartography by The Map Studio
Index by Glyn Sutcliffe
Picture research by Image Select International
Origination by Grasmere Digital Imaging, Leeds, UK
Printed and bound in China by L. Rex Printing Company Ltd.

02 03 04 05 06   10 9 8 7 6 5 4 3 2 1

For a complete list of titles available from Osprey Publishing
please contact:

Osprey Direct UK, PO Box 140,
Wellingborough, Northants, NN8 2FA, UK.
Email: info@ospreydirect.co.uk

Osprey Direct USA, c/o MBI Publishing,
PO Box 1, 729 Prospect Avenue,
Osceola, WI 54020, USA.
Email: info@ospreydirectusa.com

www.ospreypublishing.com

Contents

Introduction

The Hundred Years' War is a term invented in the mid-19th century for the late medieval conflict between England and France, although the actual war lasted for 116 years, from 1337 to 1453. England and France had been at war on several occasions before 1337 because of the tenurial relationship of their rulers. The kings of England were dukes of Aquitaine, an important area of south-west France from which most of England's wine was drawn, but they were not sovereign there, as they held the duchy of the king of France. What seems to mark out the war that started in 1337 as different is that it involved a claim by English kings for the crown of France.

Historians have long debated the seriousness of Edward III's intentions when

The term 'Hundred Years' War' emerged within a nineteenth-century context where the Middle Ages typified romance and chivalry. This is reflected in this painting of Prince Albert and Queen Victoria as Edward III and Queen Philippa at a costume ball in 1842. (Victoria and Albert Museum)

he declared himself king of France at Ghent in 1340. Did he really intend to make himself king? Or was he merely trying to use his hereditary rights as a *potential* claimant to the French throne as a bargaining counter, to win a breakthrough in the disputes that had plagued him and his predecessors over their French lands? This possibility seems to gain validity by the fact that Edward did give up his title 'king of France' in the Treaty of Brétigny/Calais of 1360 in return for a territorial settlement in his favour. Given his apparent willingness to abandon the title, can we take seriously his resumption of it in 1369 when Charles V of France reopened the war by exploiting loopholes in the treaty of 1360? The English did so badly over the next 30 years that it is hard to see the claim as anything more than an empty threat.

Yet Edward III's successors, Richard II, Henry IV and Henry V, did call themselves king of France and were all involved in conflict with France. Did they have as their principal war aim the crown of France? Was this what prompted Henry V's celebrated invasion of 1415? If so, why was he prepared to give up the title at the Treaty of Troyes in May 1420? But why, too, were the French prepared to accept him at that moment as heir and regent of their ruler, Charles VI, thereby disinheriting Charles's own son (later Charles VII) and paving the way for a double monarchy of England and France – a prospect as remarkable at the time as it might seem to us now?

As it happened, Henry V died a few weeks before Charles VI in 1422. Thus it was his nine-month-old son, Henry VI, who became king of both kingdoms. He was crowned as king of England at Westminster Abbey in November 1429, and as king of France at Notre Dame in Paris in December 1431. His crowning might suggest that the English had won the Hundred Years' War. But the victory was short-lived. Neither a treaty nor a coronation could make the French accept a ruler who was king of their bitterest enemies.

In 1429 the tide began to turn, partly as a result of the triumphs of Joan of Arc, which add a remarkable, and still not wholly explained, dimension to this stage of the Hundred Years' War. By 1450 the English had been expelled from their last remaining stronghold in Normandy, and in 1453 Gascony also fell. Only Calais, taken by Edward III in 1347 in the wake of his victory at Crécy in 1346, remained in English hands, hardly enough to justify the retention of the title 'king of France'. Yet English kings did retain this title down to 1801, two and a half centuries after they lost their last toehold in France – Calais, in 1558.

The Hundred Years' War raises many problems over the war aims of the English kings and of French responses to them. It is also an intriguing war in military terms, not least because of what it suggests about the development of infantry and artillery, which some have deemed to constitute a veritable 'military revolution'. The Hundred Years' War contains many different styles of warfare: naval and terrestrial; sweeping, long-distance *chevauchées* (mounted raids); systematic conquest and occupation; 'set-piece' sieges and battles, as well as short, sharp periods of *blitzkrieg*; small-scale skirmishes and 'unofficial' raiding and piracy. Although it was fought predominantly in France, England was itself a theatre because of raids on the south coast by the French and on northern England by their allies, the Scots.

There can be no doubt, too, that the Hundred Years' War plays a fundamental part in the formation of both England and France as nation states. Taxation developed in order to finance the war. The demand for an effective military machine helped to create complex administrative structures and moves towards standing armies. There is nothing like a war, especially a long-drawn-out one, to promote a sense of awareness of national identity and unity. With English governments frequently reminding their subjects that the enemy French were intent upon invading and destroying the English tongue, it is not surprising that this tongue should be extolled, and the sense of Englishness thereby enhanced. Although wars in this period were still basically caused by, and fought over, the rights of kings, there can be no doubt that the Hundred Years' War was waged between the peoples of both kingdoms, not least because the rulers made it so.

The coronation of Henry VI as king of France. This took place in Notre Dame in Paris on 16 December 1431. The king had celebrated his tenth birthday on 6 December. (British Library)

A hundred years is a long time, even in the medieval period where, without the benefits of modern communication methods, events took longer to be known outside the area in which they had occurred. Whilst we can identify broad themes and long-term consequences, it is also essential to emphasise the various phases of the war. But even this disguises the momentous changes in the fate of whole nations which might occur as the result of one event – not least, for instance, the few hours on 19 September 1356 which saw the capture of John II at Poitiers, and led to the English triumph in the Treaty of Brétigny/Calais of 1360, or the murder of John the Fearless, Duke

of Burgundy, on 10 September 1419 by the Dauphin's supporters, which led to Henry V's acceptance as heir and regent of France in the Treaty of Troyes of 1420.

At a more local, small-scale level, individual French villages might well regard the brief but often cataclysmic passage of English troops or of the free-booting *routiers* as their defining moment of the Hundred Years' War, the kind of microcosmic detail that is necessarily lost in a book of this length. The aim here is to provide an overview of the war as a whole.

Chronology

1204–05 Philip II conquers Normandy, Maine and Anjou

1259 Treaty of Paris between Henry III and Louis IX; homage paid for Aquitaine

1294–98 War between Edward I and Philip IV

1295 Franco-Scottish alliance

1324–27 'War of Saint-Sardos' between Edward II and Charles IV

1328 Death of Charles IV; crown passes to his cousin, Philip VI

1329 Edward III pays homage to Philip

1333 Edward defeats Scots at Halidon Hill

1336 Pope Benedict XII cancels Philip's crusade; Philip demands Edward surrender Robert of Artois

First phase

1337 Philip VI declares Edward's lands confiscate

1339 Edward invades the Cambrésis

1340 Edward allies with Flemish and declares himself king of France; French fleet defeated at Sluys; Edward besieges Tournai

1341–42 Opening of Breton theatre

1346 Edward defeats French at Crécy

1347 Calais falls to Edward after 11-month siege

1355 Black Prince's *chevauchée* through Languedoc

1356 Black Prince captures John II at Poitiers

1359 Edward III attempts to take Reims

1360 Treaty of Brétigny/Calais gives Edward lands in full sovereignty

Second phase

1369 Charles V declares Edward III's lands confiscate

1369–74 French recover all save Gascony and Calais

1372 English fleet defeated off La Rochelle

1382 French defeat Flemish townsmen at Roosebeke

1389 Truce agreed, extended in 1396 to 28 years

Third phase

1412 Henry IV sends army to assist Armagnacs

1415 Henry V takes Harfleur and defeats French at Agincourt

1417–19 Conquest of Normandy

1419 Assassination of John, Duke of Burgundy

1420 Treaty of Troyes makes Henry V heir and regent of France

1423 Anglo-Burgundian victory at Cravant

1424 English victory at Verneuil

1425–28 English take Maine and move towards Loire

Fourth phase

1429 French raise siege of Orléans and defeat English at Patay; Charles VII crowned at Reims

1431 Henry VI crowned in Paris

1435–36 Burgundy defects to France; the pays de Caux and Paris fall to French

1444 Truce of Tours

The end of the war

1449 English take Fougères; French begin reconquest of Normandy

1450 French victory at Formigny

1451 Gascony falls to the French

1453 English defeated at Castillon

England and France at peace and war: 1259–1328

Enmity between the kings of France and England arose because of the landholdings of the latter in France. These were at their greatest extent between 1154 and 1204 when the Angevins ruled Normandy, Maine, Anjou, Touraine, Poitou and Aquitaine. By 1224, all save Aquitaine had been lost to the French. The Capetians had conquered the lands by exploiting their feudal overlordship.

The Angevin kings were not sovereign in their French lands but held them as vassals of the French king. This was reinforced by the Treaty of Paris, which Henry III made with Louis IX in October 1259. Henry surrendered his claims to lost lands in return for confirmation of his tenure of Bordeaux, Bayonne and their hinterland known as Gascony, and the promised reversion of other areas of the old duchy of Aquitaine, most notably Saintonge to the north of the Gironde, and Agenais and Quercy on the eastern frontier, as well as rights in the three dioceses of Périgueux, Cahors and Limoges. As some of these areas had been in French hands for over 50 years, boundaries and allegiances were doubtful. A further complication was introduced when the county of Ponthieu, the territory around the mouth of the Somme, came to the English king in 1279 through Edward I's wife, Eleanor of Castile.

The most important aspect of the Treaty of Paris of 1259 was that it confirmed the vassal status of the English kings, obliging them to pay homage to the French king for their continental lands. Henry III set the precedent, kneeling before Louis IX in the garden of the palace on the Ile de la Cité, close to the newly constructed Sainte-Chapelle.

The Sainte-Chapelle, part of the royal palace complex on the Ile de la Cité in Paris, was built by Louis IX between 1246 and 1248 to house a relic of the Crown of Thorns. (AKG Berlin)

And for what he shall give us and our heirs,
we and our heirs will do him and his heirs, kings
of France, liege homage, for Bordeaux, Bayonne
and for Gascony and for all the lands that we
hold beyond the English Channel … and we will
hold of him as a peer of France and as Duke of
Aquitaine. (Treaty of Paris, 1259)

Homage was due at every change of
monarch on either side of the Channel, and
was renewed in 1273, 1285, 1303, 1308,
1320 and 1325, albeit often reluctantly on
the part of the English king. The latter –
sovereign in his own kingdom, yet a vassal
in his continental dominions – was at a
disadvantage. His French overlord could hear
appeals by his own vassals against his rule
and could summon him to his court in Paris.
The last quarter of the 13th century saw
the theory and practice of kingship develop
by leaps and bounds on both sides of the
Channel. Edward I sought to assert his
sovereignty over vassal rulers of Wales and
Scotland. Philip IV attempted to extend his
royal authority over his subjects as a whole
and over his major vassals, in particular the
King of England and the Count of Flanders,
ruler of a rich and highly urbanised area in

A general view of Cahors, one of the cities where
Louis IX had passed his rights to Henry III as a result
of the Treaty of Paris of 1259.

northern France with important trading links
with England. Thus, just as war had broken
out in 1202 when Philip II declared John's
lands confiscate, so wars arose between Philip
IV and Edward I in 1294, and between Charles
IV and Edward II in 1324 in the same way.

The war of 1294–98

Both these wars arose out of charges
trumped up by the French. Philip
encouraged appeals from Edward's vassals in
Aquitaine. The actual *casus belli* arose from
disputes between sailors of Normandy and
Gascony, culminating in an attack on La
Rochelle by sailors from Bayonne in May
1293. In October, Philip summoned Edward
to answer complaints against his Gascon
subjects and officials. His non-appearance
and the failure of negotiations led to the
confiscation of the duchy in May 1294.
The French were already well prepared for
invasion. After a series of successful sieges,

Bordeaux itself fell, although Bourg and Blaye held out, being assisted by an armed fleet from England. Bayonne also fell briefly but was also recovered, thenceforward becoming a base for raids into the Languedoc towards Toulouse which have similarities with the *chevauchée*-style activities of the Hundred Years' War. Toulouse was one of several bases where armaments were being gathered. In 1295, Philip even planned an invasion of England.

These are not the only ways in which the war of 1294–98 presages the Hundred Years' War. In both, the defence of Gascony relied on the inhabitants of the area, and relatively few English troops were sent. Edward I did not fight in Gascony in person, choosing instead

The gateway of Libourne, a fortified town in Gascony named after Roger de Leybourne, who had been Henry III's lieutenant in Aquitaine between 1269 and 1272. (Michael Hughes)

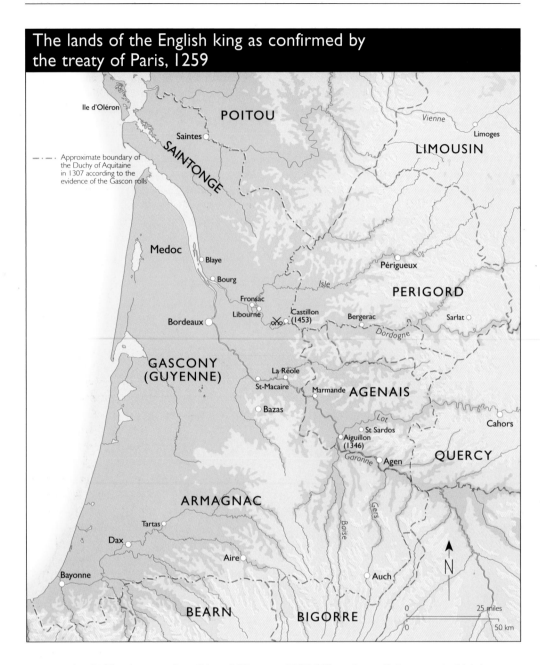

The lands of the English king as confirmed by the treaty of Paris, 1259

Ile d'Oléron

POITOU

Vienne

Saintes

Limoges

LIMOUSIN

— · — · Approximate boundary of
the Duchy of Aquitaine
in 1307 according to the
evidence of the Gascon rolls

SAINTONGE

Medoc

Blaye

Périgueux

Bourg

Isle

PERIGORD

Fronsac

Libourne   Castillon
            (1453)   Bergerac   Sarlat

Bordeaux

Dordogne

GASCONY
(GUYENNE)

La Réole

St-Macaire   Marmande AGENAIS

Bazas

Lot

St Sardos   Cahors

Aiguillon
(1346)

Garonne   Agen   QUERCY

ARMAGNAC

Gers

Tartas

Baise

Dax

Aire

N

Bayonne   Auch

BEARN   BIGORRE

0   25 miles

0   50 km

to campaign in Flanders, much as Edward III was to do later. Indeed, no king of England went to Gascony throughout the whole of the Hundred Years' War.

Secondly, although the war of 1294–98 was not dynastic, it showed that Anglo-French war had to be waged on a grand scale, as a conflict between monarchs with much pride at stake. Thus costs were immense even though the actual war was short. Philip spent at least

£432,000, perhaps 61.5 per cent of his income for 1294–98. He tied up large sums in sieges and occupation of castles, many of which changed hands with alarming frequency, much as they were to do after 1337. Edward spent around £400,000 – all of his regular and taxation income. He had to have recourse to a very heavy customs duty, the *maltolte* (evil tax), facing much criticism. He desperately needed funds to repay loans – as with his successors, there was never enough ready cash. The nobility opposed his demands for military service when he was not campaigning in Gascony in person. Thus at Ghent on 5 November 1297 he was forced to reissue Magna Carta and to abandon the *maltolte*, confirming the need to have parliamentary approval for the levy of taxation, a major turning point in English history.

Henceforward no aids, mises or prises will be taken from the kingdom except by the common consent of the whole kingdom and for the common benefit of the kingdom. (Edward I's agreement of 5 November 1297)

Thirdly, Edward I sought to divert Philip by campaigning in northern France with the aid of alliances of Low Country and German princes eager to be paid for their military services, and often with their own axes to grind against the French. Flanders was particularly ripe ground for this strategy in the late summer of 1297. A similar policy was adopted by Edward III in the early stages of the Hundred Years' War, and the negotiation of alliances remained a major feature throughout the conflict.

There is a further 'international' area where the war of 1294–98 set the scene: the development of the Franco-Scottish link, the 'auld alliance'. Indeed, it was because Edward tried to impose his lordship over Scotland by summoning John Balliol, whom he had chosen as king in 1291, to provide military service, that Anglo-Scottish relations broke down and that a Franco-Scottish treaty arose in October 1295. From this point Edward was also at war with Scotland, a war that dragged on inconclusively into the next century. Whilst some advances were made, these were lost under Edward II when the Scots, now under the rule of Robert I (Bruce), defeated the English at Bannockburn (1314), an important victory for infantry over cavalry, and began to launch raids into England. It was already clear that Anglo-French wars would not simply be a straight fight between these kingdoms.

A truce came about in 1298. In May 1303 a second Treaty of Paris restored Edward's lands.

The sting was taken out of the payment of homage by him bestowing the duchy on his son, Edward, Prince of Wales (later Edward II). It was the latter who paid homage in 1308, and whose marriage to Philip IV's daughter, Isabella, was intended to cement peace between the two sides. At this stage, no one could have envisaged that this marriage was to lead to its offspring, Edward III, being in a position to claim the crown of France. Philip IV had three sons, thus the French succession seemed unproblematic.

The war of 1324–27

The war of 1294–98 exacerbated the problems of sovereignty and territory. There were also new disputes, not least over the restitution of lands that had fallen into French hands between 1294 and 1303. A conference was held at Périgueux in 1311 but to little avail. Pressure on the frontiers of the English lands continued. These factors contributed to the outbreak of another war in 1324.

Again, the war was provoked by the French. Charles IV's officials encouraged the abbot of Sarlat to build and fly the French flag at the *bastide* of Saint-Sardos in the Agenais, an area technically under English rule, but which had been disputed since the war of 1294. Charles was perhaps anticipating that the English military response would be constrained by commitments in Scotland. The English seneschal of Gascony, Sir Oliver Ingham, took the bait. He attacked the *bastide*, allowing Charles to summon Edward to his court, and subsequently confiscate his lands.

Charles IV himself journeyed down to Toulouse – a rare visit of a French king to the south – where the nobility of the Languedoc gathered in arms in his support. Ponthieu fell without resistance. The French took the Agenais and laid siege to La Réole. The war cost the English much less than that of 1294, but there was marked expenditure on defensive engines at Bordeaux aimed at keeping enemy shipping at bay. The French took few places in Gascony thanks to local forces aided by English and Aragonese troops.

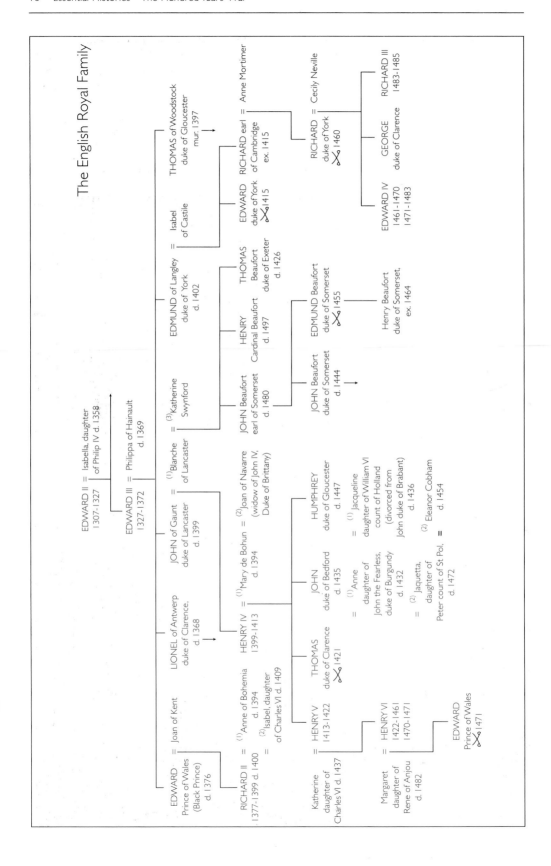

The English Royal Family

EDWARD II = Isabella, daughter
1307-1327   of Philip IV d. 1358

EDWARD III = Philippa of Hainault
1327-1372   d. 1369

EDWARD = Joan of Kent
Prince of Wales
(Black Prince)
d. 1376

LIONEL of Antwerp
duke of Clarence,
d. 1368

JOHN of Gaunt
duke of Lancaster
d. 1399

(1) Blanche
of Lancaster
=

(3) Katherine
Swynford
=

EDMUND of Langley
duke of York
d. 1402

= Isabel
of Castile

THOMAS of Woodstock
duke of Gloucester
mur. 1397

RICHARD II = (1) Anne of Bohemia
1377-1399 d. 1400   d. 1394
= (2) Isabel, daughter
of Charles VI d. 1409

HENRY IV = (1) Mary de Bohun
1399-1413   d. 1394
= (2) Joan of Navarre
(widow of John IV,
Duke of Brittany)

JOHN Beaufort
earl of Somerset
d. 1480

HENRY
Cardinal Beaufort
d. 1447

THOMAS
Beaufort
duke of Exeter
d. 1426

EDWARD   RICHARD earl = Anne Mortimer
duke of York   of Cambridge
⚔ 1415   ex. 1415

RICHARD = Cecily Neville
duke of York
⚔ 1460

HENRY V
1413-1422

THOMAS
duke of Clarence
⚔ 1421

JOHN
duke of Bedford
d. 1435

= (1) Anne
daughter of
John the Fearless,
duke of Burgundy
d. 1432
= (2) Jaquetta,
daughter of
Peter count of St Pol,
d. 1472

HUMPHREY
duke of Gloucester
d. 1447

= (1) Jacqueline
daughter of William VI
count of Holland
(divorced from
John duke of Brabant)
d. 1436
(2) Eleanor Cobham
= d. 1454

JOHN Beaufort
duke of Somerset
d. 1444

EDMUND Beaufort
duke of Somerset
⚔ 1455

Henry Beaufort
duke of Somerset,
ex. 1464

EDWARD IV
1461-1470
1471-1483

GEORGE
duke of Clarence

RICHARD III
1483-1485

Katherine
daughter of
Charles VI d. 1437
=

HENRY VI = Margaret
1422-1461   daughter of
1470-1471   Rene of Anjou
d. 1482

EDWARD
Prince of Wales
⚔ 1471

Actual war was conducted for only 15 months. In October 1325 Edward, Prince of Wales (the future Edward III), accompanied by his mother, paid homage to Charles at Paris. Whilst negotiations continued, Queen Isabella returned to England with her son and engineered the deposition of her husband in January 1327. This was facilitated by the armed support of John of Hainault, acquired through the marriage of his brother the Count's daughter, Philippa, to Prince Edward. This link was to be important in Edward III's search for allies at the outset of the Hundred Years' War.

Edward III ordered a magnificent tomb for his father Edward II, in Gloucester. The effigy, in alabaster, was intended to emulate the marble effigies of the French kings in the abbey of Saint-Denis. (Published with the consent of Gloucester Cathedral Chapter)

In February 1327 the English were still urging the seneschal of Aquitaine to recruit Aragonese troops, whilst the French were considering plans for a full-scale invasion of the duchy. An interesting document survives in the papers of one of Charles IV's councillors estimating that a 14-month campaign would be required, and that the cost could be over three times the annual average income of the French crown. It would be impossible, therefore, without exceptionally heavy taxation, a problem that beset both sides throughout the Hundred Years' War. But what is significant is that the French were contemplating the complete removal of the English only a decade before the Hundred Years' War began.

The deposition of Edward II and the accession of his son at the age of 14 made it difficult for the English to avoid agreeing to peace terms not in their favour. The French were in no real position to conquer Gascony, but they still had the military upper hand: even as negotiations went on, sieges were being conducted along the Dordogne. The peace of Paris agreed in March 1327 and proclaimed in September forced Edward to pay a war indemnity of 50,000 marks as well as a relief of 60,000 livres tournois for the duchy, for which he had already paid homage in 1325. Worse still, the Agenais remained in French hands, as did the area around Bazas. Disputes over the lands of dispossessed Gascons dragged on inconclusively.

England, Scotland and the French crown

In the meantime, the English attempted to renew war against the Scots but failed to encircle them as they penetrated into Weardale in July 1327: the English campaign was marred by a violent dispute between John of Hainault's company and English archers. Under such circumstances, Edward III and his advisers had little choice but to agree to another humiliating settlement. On 17 March 1328 at the Treaty of Edinburgh (confirmed at Northampton in May) Edward surrendered 'any right in Scotland which we and our ancestors have sought in past times in any manner', thereby recognising Robert I as king of Scotland without requiring any homage.

Into this scenario came a new issue, the succession to the crown of France. Charles IV died on 31 January 1328. All had to await the birth of Charles's posthumous child (1 April 1328). This turned out to be a girl. An assembly had already decided in February 1317 that women could not succeed to the kingdom of France. (This decision had been occasioned by the potential inheritance of the daughter of Louis X, who was passed over in favour of her uncle, Philip V.) Thus there was little debate in 1328. The rightful heir had to be Philip of Valois, the deceased king's cousin, who had acted as regent whilst awaiting the birth of Charles's child.

The *Grandes Chroniques de France* tell us that an English delegation did come to Paris to argue that Edward III, as nephew, was the nearer relative of Charles than Philip as cousin. Some French lawyers may even have agreed, but there was counter argument that Edward's claim was weakened by coming through a woman and by his status as a French vassal. The matter was effectively closed by Philip's crowning at Reims on 29 May.

It was also argued that it had never been known and envisaged that the kingdom of France should be submitted to the government of the king of England, and that the latter was a vassal and liege man of the king of France. (*Grandes Chroniques de France*, on the accession of Philip VI)

It is difficult to know how seriously the English took the matter of the claim to the French throne in 1328. No effort seems to have been made at that point to use it to negotiate better terms over Gascony. What we can be certain about, however, is that the year 1328 was momentous for both countries. Each had a new king whose title to the throne was unusual, although not suspect. The outbreak of the Hundred Years' War is linked to how Philip VI and Edward III tried to assert their authority at home and abroad in the decade that followed.

The French Royal Family

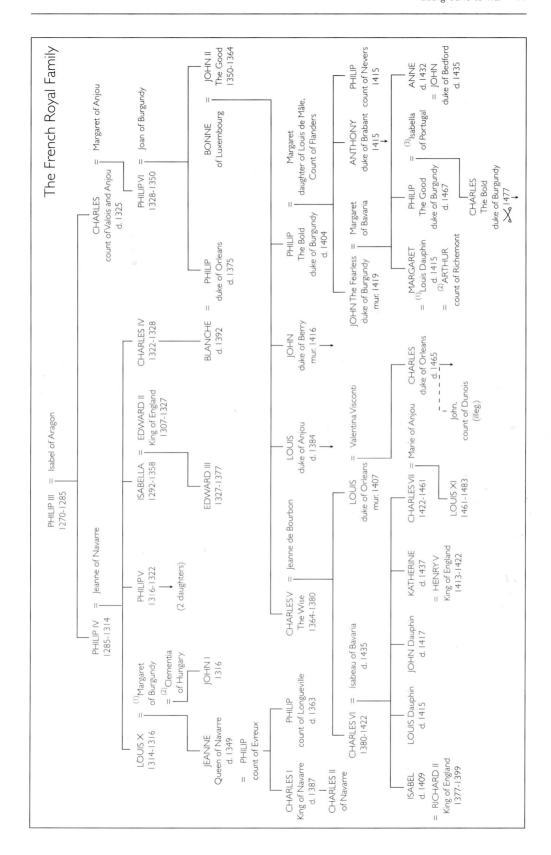

The English and French monarchies on the eve of the Hundred Years' War

Edward III and Philip VI

Although both kings were secure on their thrones, their mode of accession – Philip by the choice of the magnates, and Edward's by the deposition of his father – created some weaknesses. The English monarchy remained weaker for longer, during which time the advantage lay with the French. At the point of their accessions, Edward was only 14, Philip 35.

Philip's position was fortified by an early military victory. The Count of Flanders, Louis of Nevers, took refuge at the French court in 1325 in the face of rebellion led by Bruges. At Philip's coronation, Louis again asked for aid. At first, Philip and his magnates were reluctant to act, mindful of the disaster of Courtrai in 1302 when the flower of French chivalry had been defeated by the Flemish infantry, but by the end of July 1328 an army had been arrayed. On 23 August Philip led his men to a cavalry-based victory against the Flemish at Cassel (half-way between St-Omer and Ypres), and Louis was restored. The matter of Flanders persisted, however, for Louis was driven out again in 1339, leaving the way open for Edward to ally with the Flemish townsmen. This led directly to Edward's assumption of the title 'king of France' at Ghent in January 1340. Louis' loyalty to Philip led to his own death at Crécy.

His confidence boosted, Philip took an aggressive stance against England, prompted by long-standing issues of vassalage as well as by an implicit desire to neutralise Edward's potential claim to the French throne. If Edward paid homage, he would thereby recognise Philip as king. Edward was vulnerable if he refused, especially when an

assembly of French nobility told Philip that he could sequestrate the revenues of Gascony and Ponthieu if Edward defaulted. Edward thus paid homage in Amiens Cathedral on 6 June 1329, fearing loss of money or, worse, an invasion of his French lands. Philip had been planning an army of 5,000 men-at-arms and 16,000 infantry in the early months of 1329; the English had responded by making plans of their own, although by no means on the same scale. Whether these preparations were more than mere posturing is difficult to tell.

The homage that Edward paid in June 1329 was deliberately limited in scope in an attempt to keep his options open. Whilst this had averted a possible conflict, it led to further pressure from Philip in May 1330, to which Edward had little choice but to succumb. Although from October 1330 he was fully in control of his own government, he could not afford a war with France. Thus on 30 March 1331 he accepted that his homage should have been liege, though he did not attend another ceremony.

I become your man for the duchy of Aquitaine and its appurtenances that I hold of you as duke and peer of France, according to the peace treaty made in the past … and then the hands of the King of England were put between those of the King of France and the kiss was give by the King of France to the King of England. This was done at Amiens in the choir of the cathedral on 6 June 1329. (Homage of Edward III, from a contemporary text)

Problems raised by the English king's tenure of lands in France could have led to conflict at any time. The French had already shown their

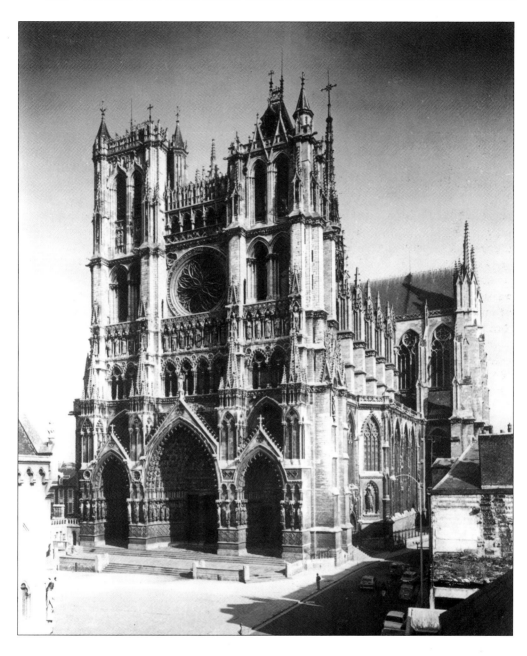

aggression, but the English were hardly likely to give up the lands without a fight. Significantly, Edward III chose to reappoint as seneschal Sir Oliver Ingham, whose actions against the *bastide* at Saint Sardos had led to war in 1324 and whose removal from office had been required by the French. Ingham proved key to the preservation of the English position in Gascony throughout, especially when war broke out in 1337. But for Edward

Amiens Cathedral, which housed a relic of the head of St John the Baptist, was chosen as a convenient and fitting location for the homage of Edward III to Philip VI in 1329. (AKG Berlin)

himself, Scotland was a more pressing issue in the 1330s.

The death of Robert I on 7 June 1329 left his five-year-old son, David II, on the throne. In 1332, Edward Balliol, son of the John who had been made king in 1291, chanced his arm with an invasion of Scotland. This may have received tacit support from Edward III. Balliol's victory at Dupplin Moor on 11 August 1332 and his subsequent crowning on 26 September encouraged Edward to offer assistance. This he did by coming north with

The effigy of Sir Oliver Ingham in Ingham church, Norfolk (early 1340s). Ingham served as seneschal of Gascony in two crucial periods, 1325–27 and 1331–43. (Ingham Church)

an army, defeating David II's army at Halidon Hill on 19 July 1333. In the following May, David took refuge in France. English armies operated in Scotland into the mid-1330s, with Edward campaigning there in person on several occasions up to July 1336.

The Franco-Scottish alliance, confirmed as recently as 1326, ensured Philip's interest in the matter. More significantly, it enabled Philip in 1334 to introduce a new demand into negotiations on the tenure of Gascony, namely that Scotland should be included in any settlement. This threatened to undermine Edward's freedom of action in Scotland, a move hardly likely to be pleasing to him when he now had a chance of reversing the defeats of earlier decades against his northern neighbours. Philip's demand was tantamount not only to preventing any advance in negotiations over outstanding problems in Gascony, but also to preventing a settlement over Scotland. A further complication here was Philip's intention to launch a crusade to the Holy Land.

Military organisation

It is at this point that we need to review the military potential of both sides. Both had recent experience of war, and thus the raising of armies was well established. In France, the king deployed his feudal rights to summon the nobility to service and to call out the population through the *arrière-ban*. In practice, the latter was often used to raise money in lieu of service. In England, these rights were less formal, but the king was able to rely on the military support of the nobility and of the shire levies. In both countries, all soldiers were remunerated with pay, such developments having begun in the reigns of Edward I and Philip IV.

There was ample armed might at the kings' disposal, although it had to be called out on each occasion and needed time to assemble. Thus response time was slow. No one doubted the king's right to wage war. All wars were portrayed as defensive, fought in defence of the rights of the ruler, but they were already wars of the king *and* his people, because the king was the defender of his subjects. His rights were their rights. This could easily be fanned by propaganda in which the churches of both countries assisted with orders for prayers for the king's endeavours. The church was already a source of royal taxation in both countries, the controversy over that being won in the face of wars from 1290 to 1310.

The potential for larger armies (20,000 or more) lay with the French because their country had a higher population. Records of a hearth tax (*fouage*) levied in 1328 suggest a total population of 12.25 million. England is unlikely to have had more than 6 million. Although France contained many semi-independent provinces, this made little difference (save in civil war) to the king's ability to raise men from a wide geographical area as troops were recruited through the nobility of the areas, as well as through towns under royal control. Actions would often see troops drawn from neighbouring locations. Thus Languedoc provided men for campaigns in Gascony, whereas troops from north of the Loire would be used in the northern theatre.

The English were at a disadvantage in that they had to bring troops over the sea. In their lands in the south-west of France, this problem was partly mitigated by the use of Gascons in their own defence, something that the large number of petty nobility in the area facilitated. Between 4,000 and 7,000 men could be raised in this way. They were pleased to serve for pay, and in defence of their land. For them, better a distant ruler in England than a French king nearer to hand. Moreover, Anglo-Gascon interests were brought closer through economic ties, not least the wine trade. There was some danger of defections to the French. Particularly significant here were the larger tenants and neighbours of the king-duke, such as the counts of Foix, Albret and Armagnac.

If the defence of the duchy needed to be boosted in the face of a major French onslaught, or if campaigns were to be launched outside Gascony, then support from England was needed. Even then, the co-operation of the Gascons was a military advantage in both defence and offence, the latter being well evidenced by their role in the Black Prince's *chevauchées* of 1355 and 1356. The English position was also helped by the rocky terrain and long frontier of their lands in south-west France. Many small fortifications held up any invading army, although places often changed hands with alarming frequency. This generated a war that tied up troops and prevented decisive outcomes. No major pitched battles occurred in Gascony until Castillon in 1453, and no king of either side ever campaigned there.

For campaigns in the north of France, the English did not have local support as they did in Gascony. Ponthieu provided no parallel in terms of troops, and was an area

vulnerable to attack, being surrounded by French territory and close to Paris. If the English were to make any impact, Edward III would have to have recourse to the policies pursued by Edward I and John, namely the purchase of alliances with rulers in the Low Countries and Germany for troops. This cost money, and also ran the risk of allies pursuing their own interests.

However, without the alliances Edward III acquired in the late 1330s (which brought 6,200 men at least), it is doubtful that he could have maintained a large military presence against Philip in the north. It is unlikely that he had more than 4,600 men with him from England in 1339. Not until the mid-1340s were systems in England amended to allow the English to field larger armies of their own. Although the military support of allies remained important throughout the whole of the Hundred Years' War, it was perhaps never again as significant as it was at the outset.

Arms and armour

In terms of armaments, there was probably little to choose between the English and the French. Already by the beginning of the war, the men-at-arms would have worn plate armour, although its quality improved over the course of the war. Infantry relied more on brigandines – cloth or leather armour reinforced with metal strips, such strips being cheaper to mass produce and easier to replace than full plate. The French did use the longbow but preferred the crossbow because it had an intrinsically longer range. Being essentially mechanical rather than dependent on man-strength, it was easier to shoot and required less training. It was thus a common weapon of the urban militias. The longbow was cheaper to manufacture, as were its arrows, since crossbow bolts had to be heavier and contain more metal. The real advantage of the longbow was that it could issue 10 shots for the crossbow's two. When there were large numbers of archers *en masse*, the longbow was a lethal weapon.

This may be the first representation of a cannon in an English manuscript. It occurs in a book of instruction for Edward III of 1326–27 and may predate slightly the similar illustration in the treatise of Walter de Milemete. (British Library)

At the beginning of the war, gunpowder weapons were scarce and unsophisticated. They did exist, as illuminations show, and were used at Sluys and in other engagements, but they were not deployed in larger quantities until the last quarter of the century, when wrought- and cast-iron pieces could be manufactured. This helps explain why the 14th-century war was largely a series of *chevauchées* and of long and abortive sieges, whereas after 1400, short, successful sieges predominated since fortifications took time to be modified against gunpowder weapons. Both before and after 1400, other kinds of siege engine were used, various throwing devices, as well as large artillery crossbows or *espringalds*, the latter also being used in defence of fortifications. Whilst English towns were not well protected by walls at this point, their French counterparts generally were.

Fighting on home soil and with intrinsically larger manpower potential, the French had the natural advantage. This was also the case with naval forces. The French kings had their own navy as well as access to Genoese galleys. The English kings were still over-reliant on the requisitioning of merchant vessels that were then provided with defensive structures and fighting platforms. Thus at the beginning of the war, English coasts and shipping were very vulnerable, and this situation was only resolved by Edward's victory at Sluys in June 1340. Ships often contained large numbers of troops, reminding us that hand-to-hand fighting was common, for the aim was to capture ships. They were too scarce and valuable a resource to destroy. Besides, until gunpowder weapons developed there was no easy way of knocking a ship out of action from a distance.

Money

The French king had the advantage in that he could finance his armies mainly from his lands, which brought in 26 tonnes of silver per annum. In the reign of Philip IV there had developed the notion of the king's right, without the need for consultation of any representative assembly, to levy tax for defence, based upon men paying for exemption from military service, but there were many exemptions, not least that of the nobility.

The English king was dependent upon taxation to boost his landed income, which lay at only 5 tonnes of pure silver per annum. Taxes on moveable property (the lay subsidy) had begun in earnest under Edward I and become virtually annual under Edward II, but needed the consent of the Commons in Parliament. This was not necessarily a weakening factor, for it enabled the king to publicise his intentions and galvanise the nation behind his endeavours. As the English nobility was smaller than that of France, the crown needed to recruit more broadly. This had already been seen in the Scottish wars, where large numbers of Welsh and English archers and foot soldiers were found, and were to be found again in the 1340s. But the armies with which Edward began the war in northern France were largely made up of nobles and their 'mixed retinues' of men-at-arms and archers, usually in a ratio of 1:1. When the English king campaigned in person, troops served for as long as he dictated. If others led his forces, then the system of indenture (contract) was increasingly used whereby conditions and duration of service could be agreed in advance.

Edward III relied very much on loans, as his grandfather had done. An important form of security was the English wool export on which finances depended in the early stages of the war. The French king was less well provided with credit systems. In 1335–36 Philip had to rely on revaluations of coinage. Shortage of money contributed to making the large royal-led campaigns short and sporadic.

The proving grounds

Recent military experience was significant. Philip had won a victory at Cassel in 1328, and was intending to crusade in the Levant. Thus he was gathering men, money and ships, as well as generating in his own mind and in the minds of his people an emphasis on military endeavour. Meanwhile, Scotland was providing Edward III's proving ground. He had experienced the difficulties of containing a raiding force in Weardale in

1327. In 1333 he had besieged Berwick, and won a victory in battle at Halidon Hill with an army of 10,000–13,000. Similarities exist between Edward's tactics at Halidon Hill and at Crécy, not least in the use of arrow fire to impede the enemy advance, although this was then followed up by a cavalry pursuit of the fleeing Scots. The victory at Halidon showed that the English could win, although the Scots were a less formidable and numerous enemy than the French in the context of a pitched battle. Rogers suggests that Edward's sweeping campaigns into Scotland between 1334 and 1336 were a precursor of his *chevauchées* in France, intended to show his military might and to bring war 'cruel and sharp' to the people who resisted his authority.

Each division of the English army had two wings of fine archers. When the armies came into contact they fired their arrows as thickly as the rays of the sun, striking the Scots so that they fell in their thousands and they started to flee from the English in fear of their lives. (Brut Chronicle on the battle of Halidon Hill)

It must not be forgotten, however, that Edward had not won his war against the Scots. He was obliged to keep some kind of military presence there even whilst fighting in France. There was always the fear of Scottish raids into England and of French aid to the Scots. The campaigns in Scotland kept the English military machine well oiled; many of those who served Edward there were to do so in France. Whilst an observer in the late 1330s might have given the French the edge in any impending Anglo-French conflict, outcomes of wars were never predictable. At base, neither side had the military capacity to defeat the other in a way that would bring a definitive victory and settlement. In this respect, therefore, the war that broke out in 1337 was already likely to last a long time and to contain many stalemates.

Mounting tensions: 1336–37

Arguably, had Philip been able to fulfil his crusading plans in 1336, Anglo-French conflict might have been averted, although it is likely that conflict over Gascony would have occurred at some point. Whether it would have arisen over Scotland is more problematic, as the French had been prone to promise military aid to the Scots but not to deliver. It seems unlikely that Edward would have gone to war over his claim to the French crown: he had already gone too far in accepting Philip's kingship. The promoting of the claim as an apparent war aim arose as a *result* of the outbreak of the Hundred Years' War, not as its *cause*. Not until 1340 did Edward declare himself king. War had already broken out in 1337 over Gascony.

An important turning point came in March 1336 when Pope Benedict XII informed Philip that his crusade could not go ahead because the problems of Gascony and Scotland had not been reconciled. 'French resources were liberated for aggressive ventures elsewhere', as Sumption puts it. In the summer of 1336, the fleet that Philip had been gathering in Marseilles was diverted to the Channel. The Scots had approached Philip for aid, and he was now thinking of sending an army there. Edward planned a short raid into Scotland in May but was afraid of doing more. A council held at Northampton on 25 June advised the sending of an embassy to France, but this did nothing to divert the French.

Edward had most to fear at this stage, faced as he was with three possible theatres – Gascony, Scotland and perhaps England itself. As it happened, Philip did not send aid to the Scots. Although Edward began to organise another campaign to Scotland, this was cancelled in November 1336. Thenceforward Edward relied on Balliol and a few English troops left for the latter's assistance. It is easy to dismiss fears of a French invasion of England in the light of hindsight, given that we know Philip never did launch a major assault. But the English government found it a useful propaganda ploy at the time of the Crécy expedition in 1346 to claim that he had so intended, sending back to England from Caen a document that purported to show the details of his plans for a landing in 1336 of 20,000 men, largely Normans, who were the maritime rivals of the southern English.

French ships carried out raids on Orford and on the Isle of Wight in the late summer of 1336, and there was plenty of panic. At a council held at Nottingham on 24 September, an array of troops for defence of the coasts was ordered. This is the point at which, to quote Sumption again, 'the English political community accepted that war with France was inevitable'. Increasingly, both nations were put on a war footing, with orders for the requisitioning of ships, the raising of loans, and the seizing of the goods of alien merchants.

Philip was already planning in late 1336 how he might invade Gascony, coming to an agreement with the Count of Foix for the service of 600 men for two months. At the same time, Edward sought allies amongst France's northern neighbours. Already he was considering possible action against Philip in northern France, either in person or through the military aid of such allies, which was crucial to him in terms of manpower. Philip's envoys were equally busy at this point in acquiring allies and limiting support for Edward.

There can be no doubt that Philip provoked the opening of actual war. In December 1336, he ordered Edward to hand over Robert of Artois, Philip's brother-in-law, who had fled from France under charges of murder. Robert's presence in

England had already been a further factor in souring Anglo-French relations between 1334 and 1336. The order to surrender Robert was delivered not to Edward in England, but to Ingham as seneschal in Aquitaine. Philip's legal authority over Edward only functioned

where the latter was duke. But Artois was in England not Gascony, and it was legally problematic whether an action by the king-

Philip VI (r. 1328–50) presiding over the lawsuit of Robert III of Artois, concerning the claim to the county of Artois. (MS fr. 18437, Bibliothéque nationale)

duke in England was within the remit of the French king. Indeed, the matter points again to the underlying problem – the tenure of lands in one kingdom by the king of another. How much influence Robert of Artois had over Edward's strategy is unclear, but some have suggested that it was he who heightened the king's awareness of the potential value of a claim to the French throne.

Arguably, Edward could have averted war by surrendering Robert. Since he did not choose to do so, we must conclude that he was willing to engage in conflict. Although in the spring of 1337 another embassy was sent to France, Edward was now making formal preparations for war. This is particularly noticeable at the parliament of March 1337 where six new earls were created, with a view to creating a cadre of military commanders. Edward still considered that armies might be needed for Scotland as well as Gascony. He may at first have intended to go to Gascony in person, but by early July he had changed his mind. It seems likely that his change of plan was caused by what he had learned of Philip's intentions.

When Philip issued the *arrière-ban* on 30 April 1337, two theatres of action became obvious, for the French armies were ordered to assemble by 8 July at Amiens as well as at Marmande on the frontier of Edward's duchy, only 50 miles (80km) from Bordeaux. A few hundred troops were sent from England to Gascony in late August. Edward took the chance that he could rely on the Gascons to maintain their own defence, under the guidance of his officials and their retinues in the duchy. Edward was now intending to join his Low Country allies for a campaign against Philip in the north, but for various reasons he did not cross to Brabant until 16 July 1338. By this time, fighting in Gascony was well under way and serious raids on England had commenced.

It is not easy to define the first action of the Hundred Years' War. There was no 'declaration of war' in the modern sense. As we saw, there were some French raids in 1336, and the Scottish theatre was in some ways already a war between England and France. But perhaps we might take the opening action as the failed attempt of one of Philip's officials to seize Saint Macaire in February 1337. Once Philip declared the *arrière-ban* on 30 April there was no turning back: he had given clear indication of his intentions to wage war on a large and national scale. The legal niceties were still to be performed. On 24 May, after Philip's council had endorsed his decision to declare confiscate Edward III's lands in France, the *bailli* of Amiens was instructed to take possession of Ponthieu. By 13 June Philip's letters declaring Aquitaine forfeit had been delivered to Edward's seneschal in the duchy, and within a few weeks French troops were launching their invasion.

The Hundred Years' War thus effectively began, as it was to end, in Gascony. It seems thus far to be following the pattern of the wars fought in 1294 and 1324. So far, too, Edward III had done no more than express his desire to defend his possessions in France and his perceived rights in Scotland. In August 1337, a manifesto was distributed to various magnates and royal officials who were to explain the King's business to meetings ordered to be held in the shires. Here Edward's reasons for the war were clearly stated: the French king had offered assistance to the Scots and usurped Edward's rights in Gascony, and had maliciously accused the latter of hindering the crusade. Significantly, there was no mention of a claim to the French crown.

[Philip] striving by all means that he could to undo the King of England and his people, so that he could keep what he had wrongfully withheld and conquer more from him, refused all offers, but, seeking his opportunities, busied himself in aid and maintenance of the Scots, the enemies of the King of England, attempting to delay him by the Scottish war so that he would have no power to pursue his rights elsewhere. (Edward's manifesto of August 1337, from the Close Rolls)

One of the most important chroniclers of the fourteenth-century
phases of the war was the Hainaulter, Jean Froissart, as portryayed in a
15th-century manuscript of his work. (Anne Ronan Picture Library)

The Hundred Years' War: a narrative

The first phase: 1337–60

Given the length and complexity of the war, it is possible here to concentrate only on direct Anglo-French conflict. It must be remembered, however, that fighting also took place in Scotland, the Low Countries and Spain, and that troops from many areas were involved. In this respect, as in the diplomatic context, it is fair to see the Hundred Years' War as the first pan-European war.

It began, like the wars of 1294 and 1324, in Aquitaine. In July 1337 the French army, which launched its attack through the Agenais, and the Count of Foix's force, which entered from the south, pursued campaigns of harassment and small-scale devastation. This is a timely reminder that the French were often as keen on the *chevauchée*-style raid as the English. This strategy was preferred when troops were few and money inadequate for long-term operations and occupation, and when war was intended to be waged on more than one front.

In 1338, the French launched further attacks through the Agenais and Saintonge. Although these were repulsed by the seneschal and his Gascon supporters, the lack of reinforcements from England meant that by the spring of 1339 the French were able to make serious inroads and were now establishing garrisons along the Dordogne and Garonne. Bordeaux was threatened with encirclement after the key outposts of Bourg and Blaye fell with the assistance of a French fleet in April 1339.

Philip intended to keep an army of 12,000 on the Garonne only until June 1339, at which point he planned to concentrate all his forces along the Somme in anticipation of the invasion of Edward and his allies. But Edward's delayed arrival led to French pressure on Gascony continuing. Siege was now laid to Bordeaux itself, but the attackers' supplies were low and they departed after only a week. Ingham was able to carry out some raids towards Toulouse in October, perhaps even intended as a co-ordinated move with Edward's invasion in the north.

The delay in Edward's crossing facilitated a number of damaging hit-and-run raids by the French on the south-coast ports. An attack on Portsmouth on 24 March 1338 was followed immediately by an attack on Jersey. The French took control of Guernsey on 8 September 1338 and held it for a few years. Although the English tried to raise a fleet against such incursions, the French were able to launch a serious attack on Southampton on Sunday, 5 October 1338.

In 1339 there were fears that Philip was planning a major assault on England from Normandy. The raid, when it came in May, was less sustained than expected, but enough to harry the coasts of Devon, Sussex and Kent. Only in July had the English gathered enough ships together to counter a planned attack on the Cinque ports. Had it not been for a mutiny of Philip's Genoese seamen, the position of England could have been much more precarious. In August the English began to take the war to the French with a raid on Le Treport, but this was too little, too late. The French had already recognised the importance of taking the war to the English, and of creating uncertainty on the coasts and in the sea lanes. In both Gascony and the Channel, therefore, the English were losing the war in its first stages.

The war in the north: 1337–39

Over the summer of 1337 Edward brokered deals with Low Country rulers for military aid, being promised almost 7,000 men, including 2,000 from the emperor, Lewis of Bavaria, for two months. These agreements served to limit Edward's freedom of action in terms of where the war should be fought. His own plan may have been to invade Normandy, with the other princes attacking France from the north-east, but the negotiations had led to an agreement that the coalition would operate together from Hainault into the Cambrésis. This served the interests of the princes and especially the emperor, under whose theoretical imperial authority Cambrai lay. But Edward was

distracted by problems in Scotland, and the assembly with his allies, initially intended for September 1337, was postponed and finally abandoned in late November. A few English troops crossed under Walter Mauny, carrying out hit-and-run raids on the Flemish coast.

That there was a lull in hostilities after this point was due to the attempted mediation of cardinals over the winter months, which led Edward to promise to refrain from an attack on France until March 1338. Nonetheless, the basic strategy of the coalition was preserved and formed the basis of the campaigns of 1338. By the end of February, Edward was raising his army of 4,500, finally crossing to Antwerp in the duchy of Brabant on 16 July 1338. This landing led Philip to order his own army to assemble on the northern frontier, with Philip himself arriving at Amiens on 24 August. But no military action ensued

because Edward found his allies reluctant to fight without receipt of pay and without the presence of the Emperor.

Edward travelled to meet Lewis of Bavaria on 5 September at Koblenz and was given the title 'vicar general of the Empire', being authorised to act 'throughout Germany and France and all the provinces and parts thereof'. Edward was now able to finalise the campaign into the Cambrésis, although the initial start date was again postponed to July 1339 as he tried to organise his finances.

Philip intended to be ready for the invasion. He placed 6,000 troops in garrisons along the border with Hainault over the winter of 1338–39, and planned to combine his military might, which was potentially as high as 50,000, by moving troops from the Gascon theatre to the Somme in the summer of 1339. The French nobility received their summons to be at Compiègne by 22 July 1339, but as Edward's invasion had still not occurred, the assembly was postponed to 6 September. Meanwhile, Edward and his allies began to assemble at Vilvoorde, beginning their march forward to Valenciennes on 18 September 1339. Exactly a week earlier, Philip had taken the symbolic banner known as the Oriflamme from Saint Denis. This was, in effect, the real opening of full war between the two kings.

Forth he fared into France ... and all his company. The noble Duke of Brabant went with him into that land, ready to live or die. Then the rich fleur de lis won there little glory. Fast he fled in fear. The rightful heir of that country came with all his knights to shake him by the beard. (The English poet, Laurence Minot, on the expedition into the Cambrésis)

Edward and his allies, with an army numbering 10,000–15,000, entered the Cambrésis, where Edward had authority by virtue of his imperial vicariate. It was no doubt deliberate that they crossed into

The city of Antwerp, then in the duchy of Brabant, which became Edward III's first base in the war in 1338–39, as he prepared to invade France with the aid of his allies.

The campaigns in Northern France

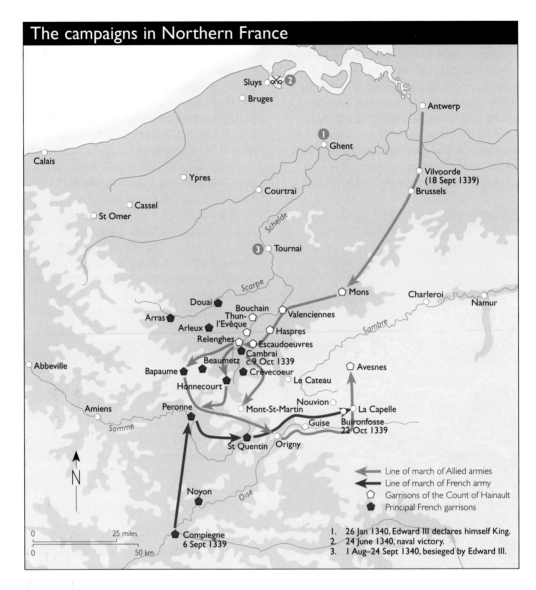

Line of march of Allied armies
Line of march of French army
◇ Garrisons of the Count of Hainault
⬠ Principal French garrisons

1. 26 Jan 1340, Edward III declares himself King.
2. 24 June 1340, naval victory.
3. 1 Aug–24 Sept 1340, besieged by Edward III.

France on 9 October, the festival of St Denis. They had few supplies with them, implying that they thought that Philip would be drawn to battle quickly. Their need to live off the land prompted considerable pillaging – a useful way, too, of undermining Philip's reputation as a defender of his people. A papal alms-giving exercise in the following year reveals that 45 villages suffered damage. Never before had French civilians been victims of war on such a scale.

The French probably intended to give battle on 14 October, but Edward was not ready and withdrew eastwards over the Oise.

A formal challenge was sent by the French for battle on 21 or 22 October. Edward accepted this, and chose his position at Buironfosse. He drew up his army in a formation reminiscent of Halidon Hill, with archers on the flanks and the customary three battles in the centre. Many were knighted by Edward, indicating that he believed battle would be given.

There is still controversy over which side decided against engagement. Sumption suggests that Philip decided to dig in to force Edward to attack at a disadvantage, but the latter refused as he was outnumbered two to one, and the French were protected by trenches. Rogers, however, suggests that it was Philip who withdrew on the advice of his council, who explained that 'if he were defeated he would lose his life and his realm, but if the enemy won, he would not have conquered the realm of England nor the lands and possessions of the other lords of England'. The campaign thus ended inconclusively, although arguably the English had shown their strength in being able to cause so much devastation unchecked. But Edward had not claimed the throne at his invasion, justifying it instead through the imperial vicariate.

The campaign of 1340

The campaign of 1340 was more explicitly linked to Edward's claim to the crown. The Flemish townsmen entered the English allegiance, prompted by economic interests and by the desire to have the rebellion against their count legitimised. Thus in Ghent on 26 January 1340, Edward declared himself king of France and henceforward waged war as a putative king of that country. Whether he believed he had any real chance of becoming king is unclear, but the taking up of the title made the war more bitter, and impossible to end without a decisive military event.

Philip's plans were to revenge himself on Hainault and Brabant, and he moved his army towards Cambrai. Edward and his allies chose Tournai just to the north to deflect this French advance, and as a pro-Flemish gesture, since this town had once been in Flemish hands. The plan was for a three-pronged attack by the Flemish militias, the Count of Hainault and other allies, and the

Edward III announced his assumption of the title king of France at Ghent in January 1340. Here he is shown accepting the quartered arms of France and England, although the costume indicates that this is a late fourteenth-century portrayal of the scene. (Bibliothèque nationale)

English (although Edward himself had returned to England in March). But the French advance was not prevented, and there was further devastation caused by the French towards Cambrai.

The situation again looked unpromising for the English, but there were two areas of success. In Gascony, the sire d'Albret decided to throw his lot in with the English, which placed the French in the Agenais on the defensive. But more significant was success at sea. Philip raised a fleet of over 200 vessels aimed at intercepting Edward when he returned with 2,000 men in June 1340. But it was instead the English fleet that caught the French in the estuary of the Zwin at Sluys on 24 June 1340. This was a complete disaster for the French, with 90 per cent of their ships being captured, and high losses of men, perhaps as high as 18,000.

This enabled Edward to resume the plan to besiege Tournai, with another army being sent into Artois under Robert of Artois. But the expedition met with disaster at St-Omer, thus weakening Edward's chances at Tournai, which he had invested on 1 August, by exposing him to the French army. The French drew up at Bouvines, site of their victory against King John in 1214. But again Philip seems to have been reluctant to engage. Through the mediation of Jeanne, the dowager Countess of Hainault, sister of Philip VI and mother-in-law of Edward, a truce was agreed on 24 September for nine months.

The opening of the theatre in Brittany

After the expiry of the truce, the balance of control in Aquitaine fell to the French, who placed 12,500 men in garrisons, but in the autumn of 1342 Ingham launched an invasion of Saintonge. It was proving difficult for either side to hold conquests for long. This unstable situation, with almost continuous military action, also encouraged the growth of informal war. Already *routiers* were as active in French- as in English-held lands.

In the meantime, Edward planned an invasion for 1341 with 13,500 troops, of which two-thirds would be archers, the first sign that he felt that he needed to boost his infantry. He intended another northern campaign but his allies were lukewarm and preferred to extend the truce to June 1342. Thus over the winter of 1341–42 Edward turned his attention to Scotland, not least because David II had returned with French assistance in June 1341.

Into this scenario a new element emerged, the disputed succession of Brittany. Duke John III, who had served in Philip's army at Tournai, died on 30 April 1341. The dead duke's half brother, John de Montfort, acted decisively in seizing the main towns. Philip was reluctant to allow him the duchy, being moved by his preference for the rival claimant, the late duke's nephew-in-law, Charles of Blois, and by suspicions, which were well founded, that Montfort had already been in secret discussions with Edward. Philip acted swiftly to recover Nantes and most of eastern Brittany, and imprisoned de Montfort in Paris before Edward decided in mid-February 1342 in favour of a campaign. Brittany then became the main focus of English military efforts, with Scotland being largely abandoned.

An advance force of 234 men was despatched under de Mauny in May, and a force of 1,350 under the Earl of Northampton in August. The latter, dug in around Morlaix, defeated an attack by Charles of Blois on 30 September 1342, which perhaps should have the credit of being the first real battle of the Hundred Years' War, although fought on a small scale and with no specific gain for the English.

Edward III himself landed in Brittany on 26 October with 5,000 men. That the king had chosen to campaign here in person is significant. The most important theatre was bound to be where the king himself was. The main focus was a siege laid to Vannes, but raiding parties were also sent out. There was chance of a battle when Philip's son John, Duke of Normandy, advanced towards Vannes in January 1343, but the French drew off.

Edward's campaign proved inconclusive because reinforcements from England were not forthcoming. So a further truce was agreed from 19 January 1343 to 29 September 1346 to facilitate negotiations under papal authority at Avignon. Brittany remained divided, encouraging a war of attrition for many years: the north and east lay under de Blois and the French, and the south and west under the Montfortians and the English.

The campaigns of 1345–47

Edward repudiated the truce in the summer of 1345, buoyed up by the homage not only of John de Montfort, who had escaped from France, but also of a renegade Norman noble, Godfrey de Harcourt. Plans were made for armies to advance to Brittany, to Gascony under Henry of Grosmont (later Duke of Lancaster), and to northern France under the king. The latter did not proceed because of

Saint-Vaast-La-Hougue, where Edward III landed his army in 1346, and where Thomas, Duke of Clarence, also landed in 1412. (Anne Curry)

The campaigns in the North 1341–59

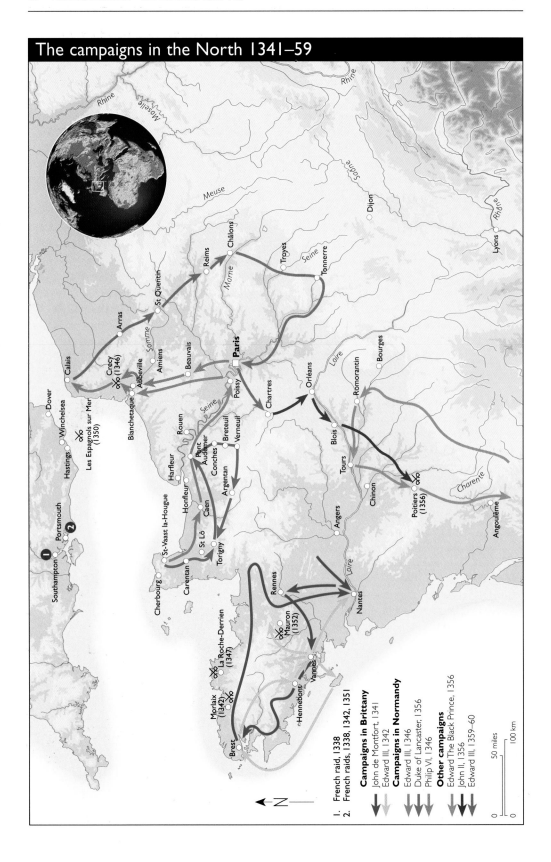

1. French raid, 1338
2. French raids, 1338, 1342, 1351

Campaigns in Brittany
John de Montfort, 1341
Edward III, 1342

Campaigns in Normandy
Edward III, 1346
Duke of Lancaster, 1356
Philip VI, 1346

Other campaigns
Edward The Black Prince, 1356
John II, 1356
Edward III, 1359–60

uncertainty of the Flemish alliance. In Brittany there was less success as sieges of Quimper (where John de Montfort died on 26 September) and Guingcamp failed, but in the following June, Charles of Blois was defeated by Sir Thomas Dagworth at Saint-Pol de Léon.

The Gascon campaign, with 2,000 men from England and several thousand locally raised men, was the first major English military effort in the duchy and led to the recapture of the important town of Bergerac. The French in their turn besieged Auberoche, but were attacked by Derby and defeated (21 October 1345). This severely undermined their attack and led to the English re-occupation of La Réole as well as penetration into the Agenais by the capture of Aiguillon and elsewhere in the early months of 1346. This was serious enough to merit the laying of siege to Aiguillon in April 1346 by the Duke of Normandy (later John II).

The position of the English was now much stronger than at any previous point in the war. The year 1346 was an important turning point not only in Edward's level of success on all fronts, but also in the kind of preparations he made for his own campaign. Gone was the reliance on allies. Now the focus was on independent action against the French, facilitated by the recruitment of an *English* army that was more securely funded.

A military assessment had been carried out of landowners based on their income. A 100-shilling landowner was to provide an archer, a £10 landowner a *hobelar* (lightly armed mounted soldier), whilst those worth £25 were to provide a man-at-arms. Many of those assessed are known to have served on the campaign of 1346 or at the siege of Calais. Others sent men in their stead, not least the older men who sent their sons. The army was boosted by those serving in return for pardons. Ayton suggests that the foot soldiers were notably undisciplined, especially at the sacking of Caen, despite Edward's order to the contrary.

It is likely that many Englishmen saw their first service in France in 1346. But how many were there? Despite a wide range of source

materials, the exact number with which Edward landed at Saint-Vaast-La-Hougue on 12 July 1346 remains uncertain. Sumption argued for 7,000–10,000, but Rogers has put the figure at 15,250, comprising 2,700 men-at-arms, 2,300 Welsh spearmen, 7,000 foot English and Welsh archers, and 3,250 mounted archers, *hobelars* and others.

This was a considerable military effort aimed at a frontal attack on Philip. It was Edward's first long and swift march of the war, setting an example that formed the basis of English strategy for the rest of the century. Caen fell to him on 26 July, but his intention was to make a show rather than a conquest: one isolated base in enemy territory would not be practicable. He chose rather to move ever closer to Paris itself, the first time the French crown had been put under real pressure.

Edward certainly intended battle. So too did Philip, but the latter hesitated when it might

Ponthieu and the campaign of 1346

To Calais
Etaples
Montreuil
Conche
Hesdin
Authie
Rue
Maye
Crécy (1346)
Le Crotoy
St Valéry
Somme
Noyelles
Blanchetaque
PONTHIEU
Abbeville
Eu
Acheux
Bresle
Oisemont
Airaines
N

0   5 miles
0   10 km

Approximate route of Edward III in 1346
Advance of Philip VI
Likely route of Henry V in 1415

have fallen more to his advantage – whilst the English were at Poissy close to the capital. Thus the encounter was on 26 August at Crécy within Edward's hereditary land of Ponthieu, and, interestingly, a place that he had visited in the pre-war period. Although the English were outnumbered (the French army numbered around 20,000–25,000), Edward's position was well chosen for both attack and defence, with his archers on the wings, and protection to the rear and sides. The French were thus forced to become over-concentrated in their attack, and to attack uphill.

Philip was impetuous in allowing his Genoese crossbowmen to engage before the rest of his army was arrayed. In fact, there was no need to attack that day, as it was already 5.00 pm when the French arrived. His folly led to over 1,500 leading French knights and nobles meeting their death, along with innumerable others of lower rank. This was a major blow not only to French pride but also to their command structures.

French realisation of the level of Edward's threat is witnessed by Philip's order of 20 August for John to abandon the siege of

Aiguillon. This opened the gates to further English success in the region, facilitating Lancaster's advance into Saintonge in mid-September, which culminated in the sack of Poitiers (4 October) where over 600 civilians died. Although the Duke did not occupy the area, his action created much insecurity and further encouraged local feuds and guerrilla warfare.

The French defeat prompted a Scottish invasion, which was overcome at Neville's Cross near Durham on 14 October. David II had taken up a position on high ground much as Edward had done at Crécy, but there were in contrast too many hedges and trees to allow him full frontal freedom. David was captured, and not released until 1357.

Edward began to lay siege to Calais from 3 September 1346. Rogers argues that this had been his objective for some time. Calais, unlike Caen, only needed defence on the land

The castle of Caen, which fell to Edward III in 1346 but was soon recovered by the French after Edward moved on towards Paris. Henry V's conquest of 1417 was longer lasting: Caen did not fall to Charles VII until 1450. (Anne Curry)

The battlefield of Crécy. The photograph is taken from the viewing platform that stands on the site of the windmill from which Edward III may have reviewed the scene. The French attacked uphill. The Black Prince's division was probably positioned below the trees on the right. (Anne Curry)

side, as it could be protected by sea from England. No longer was Edward willing to rely on his Low Country allies for a regular entry point into France. The siege was a major effort for both sides. Indeed, Rogers suggests that it was the largest single military operation undertaken by the English until the modern period. For Edward, 32,000 man-units were employed until the surrender on 4 August 1347, although the exact numbers there at any one time are not clear. Again these were English troops, around half of them archers, assisted by English ships in blockade. Philip took the Oriflamme on 18 March 1347, and contemplated engaging the besieging army, but he hesitated too long. By July, the English were exceptionally strong, and Philip departed without giving battle. Edward was free to develop Calais as a naval and military base, repopulating it with Englishmen.

A further success arose in Brittany. There Charles of Blois trying, like David II, to create a diversionary tactic, laid siege to La Roche Derrien in late May 1347, keen to draw Thomas Dagworth to battle. But the plan misfired, and in a hard, hand-to-hand fight, Blois was captured.

Further military action was threatened but both Edward and Philip were suffering from war exhaustion. Thus a papally mediated truce intervened, and the Black Death prevented further action for a while, although the informal actions in the south-west never *stopped* abated. In August 1349 the French broke the truce with an invasion of Saintonge and Poitou against English-held fortresses. In December, Lancaster responded by a counter-move down the Garonne into the Agenais and Languedoc towards Toulouse, during which many villages were burned. This may have served as an inspiration for the Black Prince's *chevauchée* of 1355.

The campaigns of the 1350s

Philip VI died on 2 August 1350. The new king, John II, carried out military reforms in 1351, ensuring that all men were within companies of between 25 and 80. Previously, discipline and command had been undermined by the tendency of men to move between retinues as it suited them. Fortnightly musters were also introduced. But a cloud was on the horizon with threats that Charles of Navarre, grandson of Louis X, and a large landholder in Normandy, might ally with the English.

The war dragged on rather inconclusively. On 29 August 1350, Edward defeated a Castilian fleet off Winchelsea, although his ramming tactics almost brought disaster.

There were many small-scale actions, such as sorties from Calais, and actions in Brittany. The south-west remained on a war footing, with both sides deploying companies a hundred or so strong to effect recovery of places. Such actions even occurred during peace negotiations directed by the cardinals. The proposed settlement, that Edward should have full sovereignty in Aquitaine, Poitou and the Limousin, reveals the perceived level of his military success to date rather than acceptance of the seriousness of his claim to the throne.

The French reneged on these negotiations. In response Edward planned another major assault. Lancaster was to lead a force to Normandy in July 1355 to ally with Charles of Navarre. But Navarre changed his mind, and

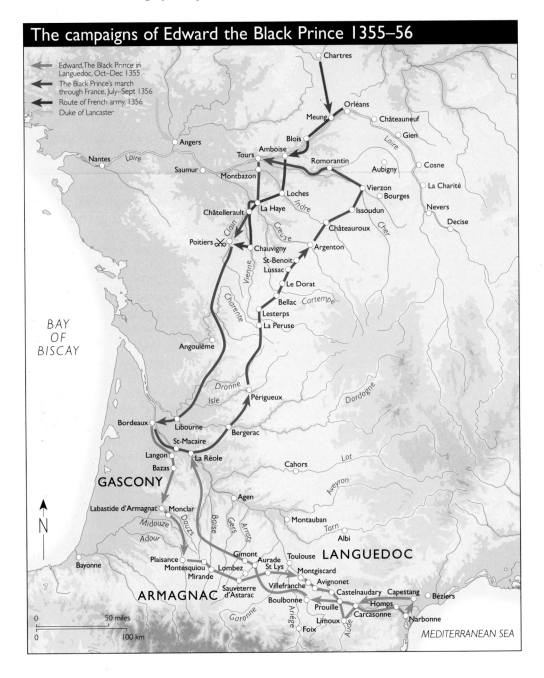

The campaigns of Edward the Black Prince 1355–56

Edward, The Black Prince in Languedoc, Oct–Dec 1355

The Black Prince's march through France, July–Sept 1356

Route of French army, 1356

Duke of Lancaster

jeban xex̃ del auu

This portrayal of John II, the first known portrait of a French king, has been dated to 1360, the year of his release from imprisonment in England. (Louvre)

More importantly, the raid of 1355 emboldened the Prince. Over the winter the English took key places as well as booty in raids up the Dordogne. By the summer of 1356 another two-pronged attack had been planned, with Lancaster landing at Saint-Vaast-La-Hougue on 18 June, to join with Charles of Navarre's brother, Philip, and troops from Brittany. An encircling *chevauchée* was conducted through Lower Normandy, with much pillaging. In the meantime, the Prince moved off from Bordeaux on 6 July with around 7,000 men, some two-thirds of whom were Gascons. His move towards the Loire was as audacious as that of 1355, but it did not prove possible to make the intended reconnoitre with Lancaster or to cross the Loire.

Thus the Prince began his return march, but found the French blocking his route at Poitiers. If he did not engage, there would be the danger of an attack on his rear as he moved towards Bordeaux. At first he

The surrender and capture of King John II at the battle of Poitiers was a great blow to the French. Here we see a fifteenth-century representation of his courteous reception by the Black Prince. (Bibliothèque Nationale)

the expedition was cancelled. Edward's own campaign to Picardy did proceed, bringing in through Calais 5,000 men to join 1,000 allies. But John II's scorched-earth policy forced an early withdrawal, and the Scottish capture of Berwick needed Edward's attention.

An army of 2,200 was despatched under the Black Prince to Bordeaux in September. The intention was to launch, with Gascon aid, a swift raid into Languedoc aimed largely at the lands of the Count of Armagnac. What made this *chevauchée*, which reached almost as far as the Mediterranean, such a success was the level of booty taken and the almost complete lack of risk. There was no French counter-attack, and the Prince wisely avoided large fortified centres. The raid did much damage to the local economy, for nothing on this scale had been seen before: Languedoc was an area previously outside the actions of the war.

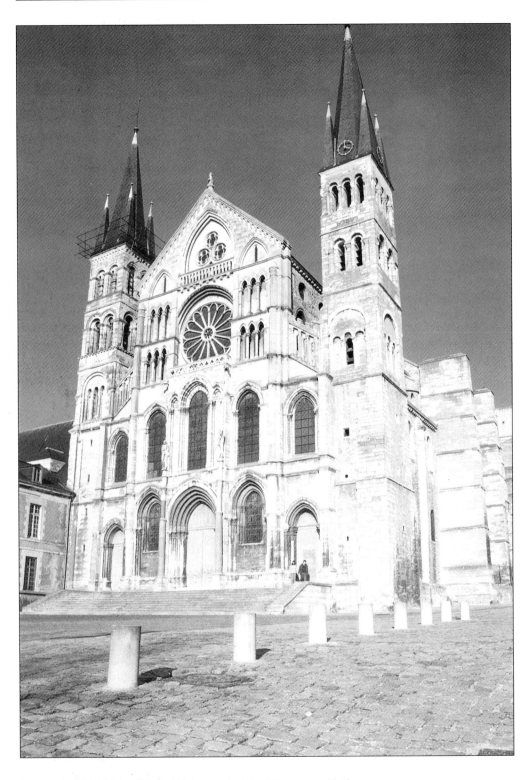

The church of Saint Rémi at Reims, which housed the holy oil that was used in the anointing of French kings, oil that was believed to have been brought by the holy spirit for the baptism of the first Christian king, Clovis, in the late sixth century. (Anne Curry)

negotiated for a withdrawal, which the French refused. Then mindful of his experience at Crécy, on 19 September he took up a defensive position on a hill, protected in the rear by woodland and by various hazards, including a hedge and marsh in front. Although the English archers again slowed down the French advance, and mowed down the first French battle, equally significant was the feigned retreat of the Earl of Warwick, which drew French troops into the marsh, and the mounted manoeuvre of the Gascon captain, the Captal de Buch, around the rear of the French army. As at Agincourt, it seems that the retreating first battle of the French collided with the second as it advanced. Thus although the French had the numerical superiority with at least 10,000 men, their weight of numbers in a confined space contributed to their undoing.

But the true importance of the battle lay in the capture of John II. This foreclosed formal military activity but stimulated informal action by demobilised soldiers as France coped with crisis and civil war between the Dauphin and Charles of Navarre. Even the English may have kept up the pressure through unofficial activity: witness, for instance, the raids of Robert Knolles in the Auvergne. When negotiations dragged in the summer of 1359, Edward decided on a massive military action aimed at taking Reims, the royal crowning place.

Perhaps this was the only time in the war that Edward seriously considered taking the French throne, assisted by the captivity of John. This would certainly explain the army of 10,000, the largest since 1347 and possibly even the largest of the reign, with which he landed at Calais on 28 October 1359. Its composition was also interesting, in that it was almost wholly mounted, containing 4,000 men-at-arms and 5,000 archers, along with 700 foreign troops. Its ratio of men-at-arms to archers was almost 1:1, a departure from his campaigns of the 1340s but similar to those of the opening of the war. Almost the whole army was recruited by indentures with captains who brought along equal numbers of men-at-arms and archers. There

was a great variation in the size of companies, from the 1,500 under the Black Prince to a company of nine under Sir Richard Pembridge.

This was the triumph of the professional 'mixed retinue', at the expense of infantry raised through the shire levies, who were needed at home in the face of diversionary raids commissioned by the Dauphin. English armies for the rest of the century followed this model.

Siege was laid to Reims on 4 December, and an assault attempted. But maintaining a long siege was well nigh impossible over the winter months. Such a large army needed too much food and was best kept on the move. But to where? Edward was unsure. There were several abortive moves towards Paris even as late as early April: this was by now an exceptionally long time to have kept an army in the field. Edward decided to call it a day, being exceptionally short of victuals.

At Brétigny near Chartres on 8 May 1360, a treaty was struck giving Edward full sovereignty in Calais, Ponthieu, Poitou and an enlarged Aquitaine. In return he would refrain from calling himself king of France. Indeed, the ransom of 3 million écus that he had accepted for John confirmed the latter's right to rule. The kings met at Calais on 24 October to confirm the treaty. The war was at an end. Edward had surely won this war, for he had gained what his predecessors could only have dreamed of – sovereign rule of half of France.

The second phase: 1369–99

Although England and France were technically at peace during the 1360s, soldiers from both countries were involved in various formal as well as *routier* activities. Civil war continued in Brittany until a force of English and Bretons under Sir John Chandos defeated and killed Charles of Blois at Auray on 29 September 1364. The French civil war with Charles of Navarre also dragged on until du Guesclin's victory at Cocherel on 16 May 1364.

But by far the most important theatre was Castile, where English and French intervened on behalf, respectively, of Pedro II and his half-brother, Henry of Trastamara. The most celebrated engagement was the Black Prince's victory at Najera on 3 April 1367, not least because of the immense logistical achievement of taking an army through the Pyrenees. The Prince's army consisted of three groups – 3,000 under Sir John Chandos and the Prince's brother, John of Gaunt, Duke of Lancaster, deployed as the vanguard, the Prince with his retinue, members of the Great Company and of Pedro's troops in the main battle, numbering another 4,000 men. The Lords of Armagnac and Albret held the right wing with 2,000 men and the Captal de Buch the left, with another 2,000. Trastamara's force was about 5,500, but was chaotically organised.

The Prince took the Castilians by surprise by using a hill to mask his advance. He was able to prevent co-ordinated action between du Guesclin and Trastamara, and to impede the latter's advance by arrow fire. But the fierceness of the hand-to-hand fighting is revealed by the wound through Chandos's visor, which destroyed the sight in one eye.

The victory enhanced the Prince's reputation but led to severe financial problems for him. The high tax that he subsequently placed on his principality of Aquitaine led to appeals to Charles V by Albret and Armagnac. This, as well as loopholes in the treaty of 1360, enabled Charles to claim the right to hear appeals as overlord and to the confiscation of English lands in November. Edward III initially tried to negotiate to avoid war, but on 3 June 1369 made war inevitable by resuming the title king of France.

It was announced that Charles, son of John, the former King of France, had usurped the sovereignty of the King of England … and had expelled him by his armies (his banners having been unfurled) from his lands in Ponthieu and elsewhere … and was still holding the same in hostile fashion, and had assembled armed ships and galleys in order to invade the kingdom of England and to overthrow the king, thus making

open war in a malicious way against his oath and against the form of peace made with the King of England. (Roll of Parliament)

In fact, hostilities had already broken out six months earlier. The French took the English undefended and by surprise, leading to early losses that made Edward's resumed royal title an empty gesture. The King's brother, Louis, Duke of Anjou, took Rouergue and Quercy in early January 1369. Relations between the Black Prince and his subjects had deteriorated so far that Gascon assistance could no longer be relied upon. Thus in January 1369 the English raised a small expeditionary force under Edward's fourth son, the Earl of Cambridge, and the Earl of Pembroke, which came to the rescue of English possessions in Périgord.

In April, the French entered Abbeville, capital of Ponthieu. The English had dispatched 250 troops there in February, but they were too few to hold the area. The fall of Ponthieu raised concerns over Calais, so that other troops intended for Gascony were diverted to Calais in May, and a new captain, Gaunt's son, the Earl of Hereford, appointed with 900 men.

Edward III realised that a major demonstration of military might was needed. He thus planned to campaign himself in northern France, and began to negotiate with allies for troops. About 1,000 men from Brabant and Juliers joined with Gaunt, who was sent ahead of his father to Calais in late July 1369 with 2,000 to counter French attacks on England. The English, not threatened for many decades, had let their home defences slip. Thus from mid-June there was a flurry of orders to fortify Thanet, Portsmouth (which was attacked in September), Southampton and Portchester, with the shire levies also being called out in July. The English launched a short raid on Sainte-Addresse, the ports of Upper Normandy being the likely place from which any attack on England would be made. There were even fears that the French might enter through Wales with the aid of the inhabitants: on 24 December, Edward instructed lords with lands there to see to their safekeeping.

The Black Prince, here portrayed on his fine tomb in Canterbury Cathedral, was
undoubtedly one of the most renowned war leaders of his age, although his rule
of the principality of Aquitaine in the 1360s was less impressive, leading as it did
to heavy taxation and appeals to the French king. (Canterbury Cathedral)

One of the problems facing the English at the outset of the second phase of the war was the increasing age of Edward III (b. 1312). He was unable to participate in the campaigns after 1369 and by the time of his death in 1377 was showing signs of senility. (Roger-Viollet)

The intention was that Gaunt should harry Picardy and Thérouanne in standard *chevauchée* style. He came close to battle with Charles's brother, Philip, Duke of Burgundy, at Tournehem on 23 August, but only a skirmish occurred. Gaunt then fell back to Calais in September. By the middle of the month another 2,000-strong army under the Earls of Warwick, March, Salisbury and Oxford landed at Calais. Edward was not with them, probably because of the death of his wife on 15 August, although he may have decided to stay in England in case the French did invade.

The actions of this composite army under Gaunt's overall command show that the English aimed to attack the areas from which invasion might come. It carried out a campaign of devastation in Upper Normandy, being assisted by the English fleet, which harried the coast. In October the army returned to Calais before the end of its contract. Gaunt had been cautious and limited in his actions, but the threat of invasion had indeed been averted.

In the following year, a more audacious move was planned. Four thousand men were contracted under Sir Robert Knolles for two years' service. The plan was to allow Knolles to emulate the activities of the *routiers*, taking pay only for the first three months and then letting his force live off the land, conducting raids when and wherever necessary. Knolles' first action was a fast and damaging *chevauchée* from Calais around the east of Paris and thence to Poitou and Brittany. But his rearguard was ambushed by du Guesclin near Le Mans, and the army disbanded only six months into its contract. Du Guesclin had already demonstrated his skill in weakening the effectiveness of the *chevauchée* by deploying his troops in flanking actions to delimit the path of the English, and to prevent any conquests.

The French under Anjou continued their advances in the south-west in 1370, taking the Agenais, Limousin and Buzac. Furious that the bishop of Limoges had entered into negotiations with the French, the Black Prince rushed to sack the city, an act most certainly against the conventions of war and chivalry. By now he was seriously ill, and returned to England in 1371, dying in 1376. The defence of English Aquitaine, or what was left of it, was entrusted to Gaunt, but only small forces of 500 and 800 men were sent for his support.

French penetration of Saintonge and Poitou prompted the dispatch of the Earl of Pembroke in April 1372 with 1,500 men and enough money to raise an army of 3,000 in Gascony. But his transport fleet had only three armed escorts to guard it, and was intercepted by Castilian galleys off La Rochelle. On 23 June, the Castilians sent flaming arrows into English ships caught in the shallows of the harbour. Virtually the whole fleet was lost. La Rochelle fell on 8 September. Equally galling was the fact that the money for the Gascon troops was at the bottom of the sea. The defeat also thwarted plans for Edward III to cross from Southampton with a force of 4,000 (the intended location of this campaign is not clear). Instead, the troops were sent to sea against the threat of further French naval action, although none materialised.

Thus in 1372 the English position already looked very bleak. There was only one glimmer of hope – a renewed alliance with the Duke of Brittany in June 1372, although this led to the confiscation of his duchy and its occupation by French troops. An advance army of 600 men under John, Lord Neville, landed there in October. It was in the following year that the English raised their largest army of this second phase, 6,000 strong, and containing the Dukes of Lancaster and Brittany as well as three earls, 12 foreign captains and nearly 250 knights. The intention was to effect a great *chevauchée* from Calais to Artois and Champagne. Not surprisingly, this caused consternation to the French, but Gaunt then decided to turn south to reinforce the position in Gascony rather than moving on Paris.

Why was no move made by either side towards a battle? Throughout this phase of the war, Charles V was not prepared to run the risk, even if this meant that English armies could raid without much constraint. There is little indication that the English were keen on engagement. The expeditionary forces they dispatched between 1369 and 1380 were all of mounted men alone, and with men-at-arms and archers in the ratio of 1:1. Thus they were more suited to raiding than to battle formation, where the lack of archers would have made them vulnerable. This contributed to the stalemate of the phase.

Stalemate also arose in the territorial position once La Réole surrendered to the French in 1374, reducing the English to the

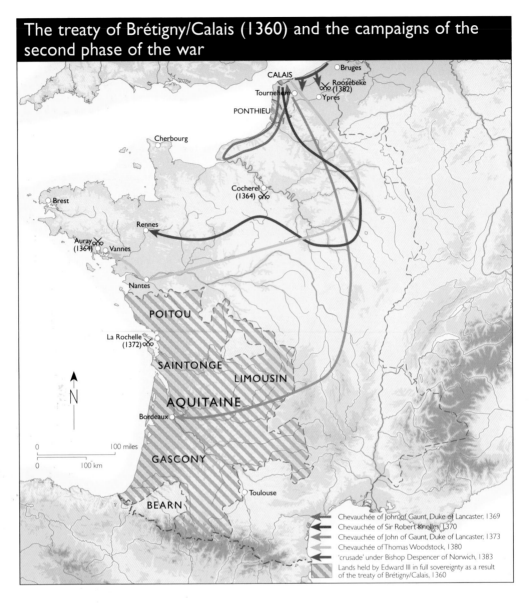

The treaty of Brétigny/Calais (1360) and the campaigns of the second phase of the war

Chevauchée of John of Gaunt, Duke of Lancaster, 1369
Chevauchée of Sir Robert Knolles, 1370
Chevauchée of John of Gaunt, Duke of Lancaster, 1373
Chevauchée of Thomas Woodstock, 1380
'crusade' under Bishop Despencer of Norwich, 1383
Lands held by Edward III in full sovereignty as a result of the treaty of Brétigny/Calais, 1360

Gascony of 1337. The sending of regular small companies from England during the later 1370s to hold the garrisons and launch occasional sorties on the frontier made it difficult for the French to penetrate further. In 1375, the English decided to concentrate their efforts on Brittany, raising an army of 4,000 under the Earl of Cambridge and the Duke. Its actions were cut short by a papally initiated truce, but when war reopened in 1377, du Guesclin and Anjou began to penetrate Gascony, besieging Bergerac. The town fell on 2 September, and other towns

along the Dordogne soon followed. Several Gascon lords defected, but Bordeaux was saved by counter-actions under John Neville.

Even so, the English position in 1377 was perhaps weaker than ever. The French launched serious raids on the south coast, facilitated by the recent establishment of a royal shipbuilding yard at Rouen. The English position was not assisted by the death of Edward III on 21 June 1377, and the accession of his 10-year-old grandson, Richard II.

Further disasters followed. A 4,000-strong force for Brittany in 1379 was reduced to 1,300 and then destroyed by sea storms off Cornwall and Ireland. In 1380, Edward III's youngest son, Thomas of Woodstock, Earl of Buckingham, led 4,000 along the, by now, customary *chevauchée* route from Calais through Champagne, Beauce and Anjou to Brittany, before laying siege to Nantes for two months without success. The Duke of Brittany came to an agreement with the

Already in a strong position against the English, the diplomatic position of Charles V was further boosted by the visit to Paris of the Emperor Charles IV in 1374. Here the two rulers are portrayed at a banquet. The scene on the right may be a reminder of hopes of a joint crusade against the Saracens. (Bibliothèque Nationale, *Grandes Chroniques de France*).

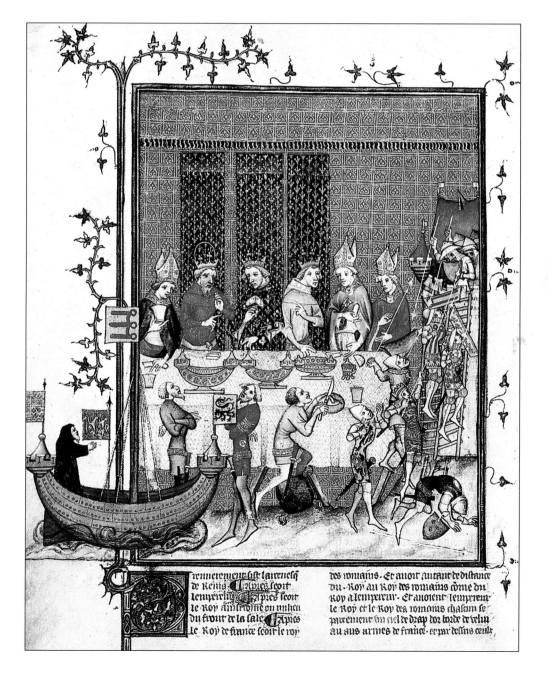

rinincrement hst laurencsh
de Reins. Apres seoir
lemperere. Apres seoir
le Roy ansewsme ou milieu
du front de la sale. Apres
le Roy de france seoir le roy

des romains. Et auoit autant de distance
du Roy au Roy des romains come du
roy a lempereur. Et auoient lempereu
le Roy et le Roy des romains chascun se
paremenr ou ciel de drap dor brode de selu
au aus armes de france. et par dessus ceulx

French on 15 January 1381, and remained largely neutral in the war thenceforward.

After 1380, the English sent no more large expeditionary forces to France: the expense that they generated had not been matched by their achievements. But a presence was maintained in Brittany, for Brest had been leased from the Duke of Brittany 'for the duration of the war with France', and Cherbourg from the King of Navarre. These usually housed 100 men, along with a good quantity of ordnance.

It was during this second phase of the war that the value of gunpowder artillery was first seen, at the French recovery of Saint-Sauveur-le Vicomte in 1375. Brest housed at least nine guns, with more brought over from England when the French laid siege in 1386. Cherbourg had 10 guns, seven firing 24-in. (61cm) stones, and three 15-in. (38cm) stones. But these were but pinpricks in what was otherwise an ever-strengthening French position, and the English failed in their attempts to take other bridgeheads in France such as Saint-Malo, Harfleur and La Rochelle. This was partly because the French had done much from the 1360s onwards to ensure the maintenance of fortifications.

After 1380, the English concentrated their military endeavours outside France. The hope of exploiting the Flemish alliance was dealt a blow by the French defeat of the townsmen at Roosebeke on 27 November 1382. The English were only able to finance an army in the following year by launching it as a crusade

against those who supported a schismatic pope. This way taxation could be levied from the church to pay for it. Bishop Despencer of Norwich's force managed to take the coast between Gravelines and Blankenberghe and to lay siege to Ypres, but the advance of the Duke of Burgundy prompted his withdrawal.

There was failure for Gaunt in Castile in 1386, and the expedition that Richard II had led to Scotland in 1385, made financially viable only by resurrecting the royal right to free service in the feudal levy, was not enough to keep the Scots at bay. In 1388, they invaded again, winning a victory in battle at Otterburn on 5 August. In 1386–87, the French laid siege to Brest. This prompted what was in effect a naval *chevauchée* under Arundel in 1387, with a further sea-borne campaign in 1388.

These were the last campaigns of this phase of the war. A short truce agreed on 18 June 1389 led in time to a 28-year truce in March 1396, cemented by the marriage of Richard II to Charles VI's daughter on 4 November. Cherbourg was handed back in 1393, and Brest in 1397. The English now held only the Gascony of 1337 and Calais.

The English military effort required in this phase was exceptionally intensive and expensive, with over 30,000 troops raised for expeditionary armies between 1369 and 1380. Evidence suggests that the armies were well organised and disciplined, yet they achieved little because of the nature of the campaigns and the numbers of theatres in which the English had to engage. The French were better prepared for attack, and had won much advantage by their swift actions in 1369. In addition to reforming company sizes and discipline, Charles V had initiated a system of provision of troops by parishes in the early 1360s against the *routiers*. This gave the French 3,000 troops on standby.

Why, then, were the French not able to effect a total victory? The answer lies in the strains that they also began to feel around

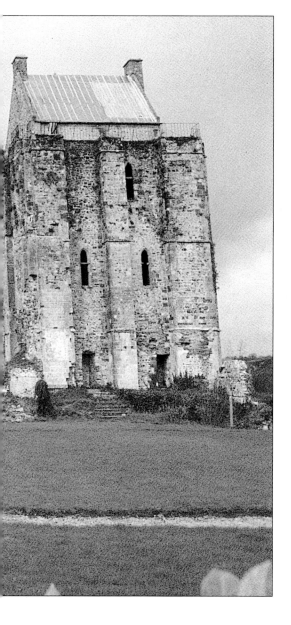

The castle of Saint-Sauveur-le-Vicomte, in the Cotentin, which was held by Sir John Chandos in the mid-14th century, and which fell again into English hands during the 15th-century occupation. (Anne Curry)

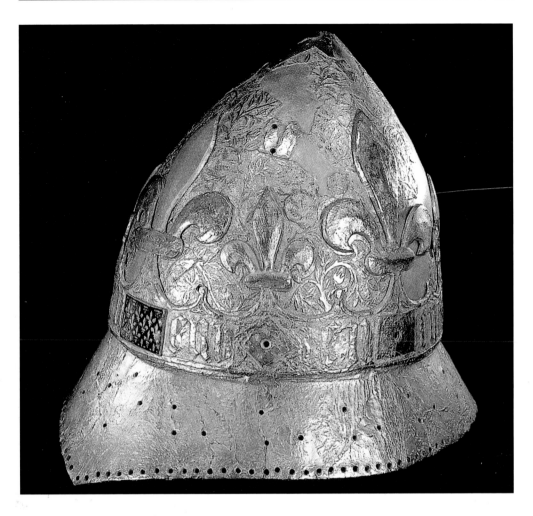

1380, with tax rebellions and increasing political divisions during the minority of Charles VI. A stalemate thus arose, in which a long truce was acceptable to both sides. This might have signalled the end of the war had it not been for the outbreak of civil war between the Burgundians and Orléanists (or Armagnacs) in the wake of Charles's growing insanity, and the change of circumstances in England following the deposition of Richard II in 1399.

This gilded parade helmet of Charles VI, dating from around 1410, belies the fact that the king, increasingly insane from 1392 onwards, was unable to play an active part in defending his kingdom or in controlling the Armagnac and Burgundian factions. (Louvre)

The third phase: 1399–1429

Although technically the truce was maintained until Henry V invaded in August 1415, the circumstances of the first 15 years of the 15th century are best portrayed as cold war. There was disquiet amongst some Gascons at the usurpation of Henry IV, but this was subdued by a small, but prompt military showing by the English. From 1403 the French launched several incursions under Louis, Duke of Orléans. Losses were incurred in the Agenais, towards Saintonge and on the frontier with Périgord. Bordeaux itself was threatened when sieges were laid to Bourg and Blaye, but these proved abortive in the early months of 1407. In November of that same year the danger receded when the Duke of Orléans was assassinated at the order of John, Duke of Burgundy.

This famous portrayal of Henry V was painted after his death. The King was aged around 28 at the time of Agincourt, but had already had several years of military experience in Wales. (Anne Ronan Picture Library)

The ensuing escalation of the French civil war made Henry IV aware that French weakness could work to his benefit. Negotiations recommenced, but, more importantly, both the Burgundians and the Armagnacs sought English aid in their own struggle. In October 1411, a force of 800 men-at-arms and 2,000 archers under the Earl of Arundel was sent to assist Burgundy at the behest of Henry, Prince of Wales.

In the following year, a full-scale army of 1,000 men-at-arms and 3,000 archers was dispatched at the King's order to aid the Armagnacs, who had promised in return to honour the terms of Brétigny. This army was commanded by the King's second son, Thomas, Duke of Clarence, accompanied by Edward, Duke of York, and Thomas, Earl of Dorset (later Duke of Exeter). All three later served in the Agincourt campaign. The army landed at Saint-Vaast-la Hougue, as Edward III had done in 1346, and carried out some raids into Normandy. It then moved towards Blois where it was to join with the Armagnacs, but was bought off when the two sides in the civil war came to an agreement. Clarence then led his men to Bordeaux before returning to England.

There can be little doubt that Henry V was encouraged in his own aggressive stance towards France by these precedents and by the opportunities offered by French internal divisions. His hard line in diplomacy was matched by his major military effort to launch an expedition in 1415. The army raised numbered over 12,000, and was notable for the extremely large number of men who indented to bring troops. This was truly the nation at war. Most of the active peerage served. The King's two brothers, the Dukes of Clarence and Gloucester, each led companies of around 1,000 men, with the royal household forming an even larger division: even men such as the surveyor of the works at the royal palaces, or the porter

A later 15th-century image of the battle of Agincourt. The artist's view of the landscape is particularly misleading as the battle was fought on flat ground that fell away only slightly on each side. (Lambeth Palace)

The Agincourt campaign 1415

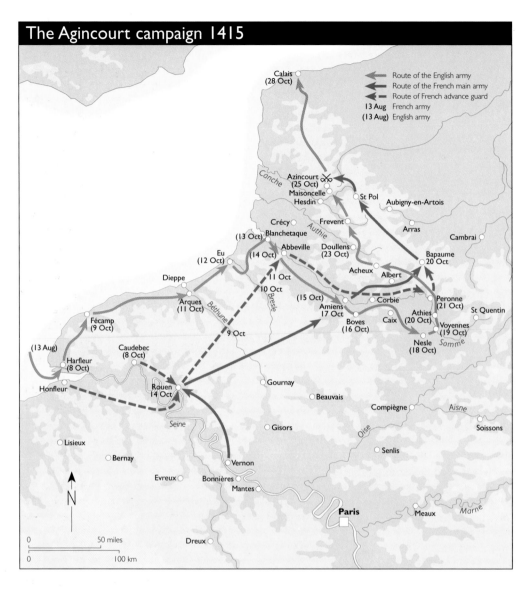

of the hall, brought along small retinues. Even more notable were the many esquires and yeomen who indented in person with a handful of archers.

The ratio of all the retinues was also distinctive, at one man-at-arms to three archers, a notable increase in the proportion of archers compared with the campaigns of the two 14th-century phases of the war. In addition, there were companies of over 500 archers from Lancashire, Wales and Cheshire, all with close links to the crown. This ratio is first seen in the campaigns in Wales. It would be tempting to say that it was testimony to the

realisation of the firepower of archers, but it was more likely moved by the fact that archers cost half the daily wage of a man-at-arms – a significant factor when Henry had cash to pay for only the first three of 12 months' intended service, and had to provide jewels as security for the following three months.

Whereas Henry IV had concentrated his efforts on Gascony, his son launched a new enterprise aimed at Normandy. It is highly likely that the first expedition of 1415 was aimed at conquest. But the siege of Harfleur took longer than anticipated and Henry lost at least a third of his army to disease and to the need to garrison his conquest. Thus a form of *chevauchée* ensued, although one aimed at showing a presence rather than taking booty, for Henry was careful to restrain his troops, perhaps because he realised the vulnerability of his diminished and weary army, not least as he was forced to march so far inland to find a crossing of the Somme.

Henry's order that the archers should prepare stakes was made in anticipation not of battle but of ambush by the French, who were stalking him all the way as well as preparing a major army at Rouen in the hope of revenging themselves for Poitiers: their army was equally lustrous in terms of the participation of the peerage, and numbered at least 20,000. But this was not to be. Although they chose to bring Henry to battle at Agincourt on 25 October, he was able to exploit the natural features of the site to funnel and limit their attack.

The French battle plan, which still survives, included an intended cavalry charge against the archers, which might indeed have taken them out. But the charge was limited, and the archers were thus able to harry the main French foot advance. Accounts of the battle suggest that the French lost their momentum, were too closely packed to use their weapons, and piled on top of each other, where they were easy pickings for men-at-arms and archers alike. The carnage on the French side was immense, with important prisoners being captured, not least the King's nephew, Charles, Duke of Orléans. Yet we must be mindful of the fact that Henry had been uncertain enough of victory to order the killing of prisoners when he feared a renewed French attack.

In the opinion of the French, it was what injured them the most which assured the English of victory, especially the continuous hail of arrow shot which rained down on our men. As the English archers were lightly armed and their ranks not too crowded, they had freedom of movement and could deal mortal blows with ease. Many of them had adopted a weapon until then unknown – great lead-covered mallets from which one blow to the head could kill a man *or knock him senseless to the ground.* (Chronicle of the Religieux of Saint-Denis)

Less remembered but equally significant for Henry's plans was the naval victory of his brother, the Duke of Bedford, over the French and their Genoese allies in the mouth of the Seine on 15 August 1416. This battle was hard fought, lasting around seven hours with high losses on both sides. But for the English it secured the safety of Harfleur, and facilitated Henry's second campaign by weakening French maritime defences. On 1 August 1417 he landed again in Normandy, at the mouth of the Touques. This time his intended systematic conquest met with complete success. Caen withstood siege for two weeks. Henry then moved south to take Alençon and other places on the frontier with Maine.

Once Falaise fell in February 1418, after a siege of over two months, Lower Normandy was divided into two by the English conquest, and Henry could divide his forces for campaigns to the west and east. The Cotentin fell swiftly save for Cherbourg, which held out for five months until September 1418. The area towards the Seine fell by mid-summer, and Henry began his siege of Rouen in late July. Rouen held out for six months, but once it was in English hands, the remainder of Upper Normandy fell with little resistance. By the summer of 1419 virtually the whole of the duchy was in Henry's hands, with English garrisons distributed in key points.

Henry had been assisted by an army in 1417 of at least 10,000, with reinforcements crossing in subsequent years. With such numbers, and with experienced commanders of high status, he had been able to employ a multi-pronged approach, thereby speeding up the conquest. His use of artillery is also notable, as defences were inadequate to resist bombardment. Henry consciously distributed lands to his soldiers, demanding in return both defensive and offensive military obligations, thus giving many a vested interest in maintaining and extending the conquest. This was a new and imaginative ploy, reinforced by his good treatment of the Normans.

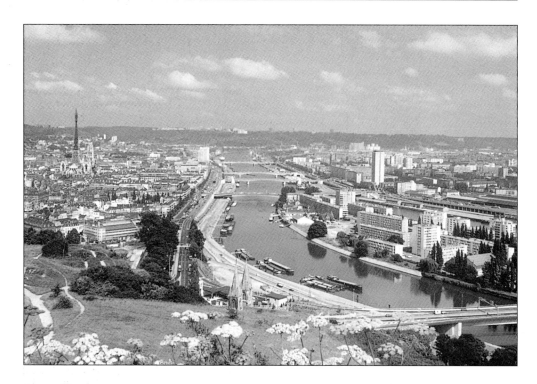

A general view of the city of Rouen, which surrendered to Henry V in January 1419, and which became the centre of English rule in France after the loss of Paris to Charles VII in 1436. (Anne Curry)

There seems little doubt that Henry's war aim was to take and hold Normandy. That was the focus of his negotiations with the French in 1419, but his ambitions were boosted when the civil war took another turn for the worse. Duke John of Burgundy had taken advantage of the English attack to take Paris in May 1418, and control of the mad king. Efforts to reconcile him with the Armagnacs, now led by the Dauphin Charles, came to nothing when he was assassinated at Montereau on 10 September 1419. This led directly to an Anglo-Burgundian alliance and to Henry increasing his war aims to the crown itself. By the Treaty of Troyes of May 1420 he became heir and regent of Charles VI.

One of the clauses of the treaty committed Henry to making war on the Dauphin and the Armagnacs until all of France accepted the treaty. This was a tall order as Henry's last two years revealed.

Even close to Paris, there were places that resisted: Henry spent most of his last years in France in sieges to the east of the capital. The siege of Meaux, his last engagement where he contracted dysentery, began in October 1421 and lasted until March 1422. The move southwards by the Duke of Clarence had led to his death in battle at Baugé on 22 March 1421, a battle that saw further important casualties and prisoners.

Henry's early demise in 1422 did not make the matter any easier. Many places supported the Dauphin. Mont-Saint-Michel, for instance, was never captured despite several sieges by land and sea, and even within Normandy and the Ile de France, the Armagnacs recovered places from time to time. The Dauphin was assisted by Scottish troops, although two major blows were served to his cause by the defeats suffered at Cravant (31 July 1423) and Verneuil (17 August 1424). The latter opened the way for an offensive into Maine, which fell to the English over 1425–28, and then to the Loire, culminating in the siege of Orléans laid in October 1428.

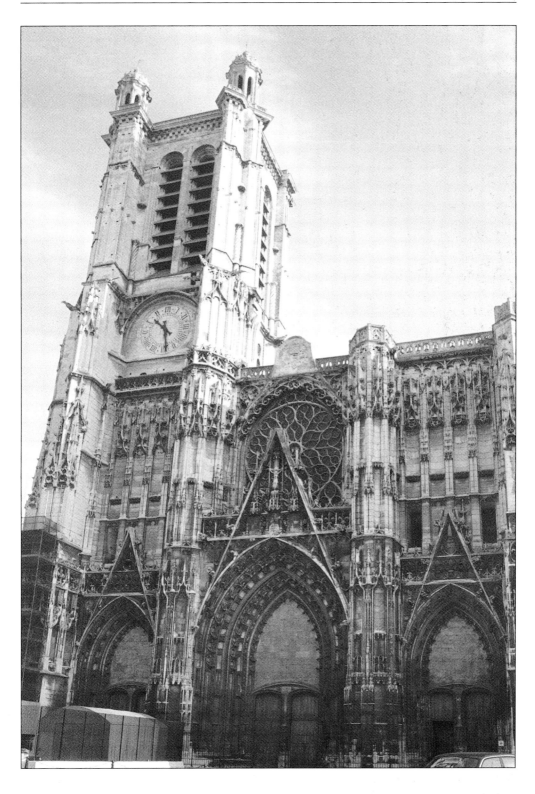

The cathedral of Troyes, where the treaty of 1420 was sealed. The marriage of Henry and
Catherine, daughter of Charles VI, took place in the church of St John. (Anne Curry)

Major campaigns 1415–28

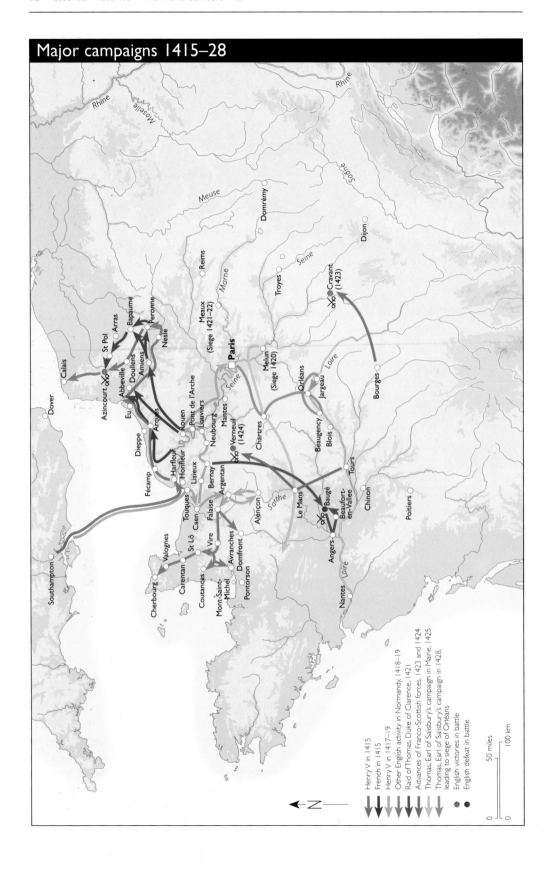

Henry V in 1415
French in 1415
Henry V in 1417–19
Other English activity in Normandy, 1418–19
Raid of Thomas, Duke of Clarence, 1421
Advances of Franco-Scottish forces, 1423 and 1424
Thomas, Earl of Salisbury's campaign in Maine, 1425
Thomas, Earl of Salisbury's campaign in 1428,
leading to siege of Orléans
English victories in battle
English defeat in battle

50 miles

100 km

The fortified abbey of Mont-Saint-Michel, which was the only part of Normandy that the English failed to conquer in the 15th-century phase of the war. (AKG Berlin)

Throughout the 1420s the English had sent regular expeditionary forces to France, and had also been able to draw on valuable military assistance from the Burgundians, who had themselves developed an impressive military and artillery presence. What is particularly notable about this period of the war is the strong defensive provision in the form of garrisons placed throughout Normandy and the other areas under Anglo-Burgundian authority. These followed the precedents laid down by Henry V, and were well organised during the regency of John, Duke of Bedford, being administered through French systems and financed through local taxation. Considerable attention was paid to the maintenance of military discipline and to good relations with the civilian population.

The fourth phase: 1429–53

The victory at Verneuil had enabled the English to scale down their garrisons as well as to extend their territory. But their advance came to an end when the French, inspired by Joan of Arc, raised the siege of Orléans in May 1429. The English had maintained a strong siege with over 4,000 men, but had been damaged by the death of their commander, the Earl of Salisbury, from a gunshot early in the siege, and by the withdrawal of Burgundian troops in April.

The French, whose numbers are unclear, now carried all before them, defeating the English in pitched battle at Patay on 18 June 1429, where the English archers were encircled by the French cavalry charge. Two leading English commanders, the Earl of Suffolk and John, Lord Talbot, were captured. The French then conducted a veritable *blitzkrieg*, capturing many places en route to Reims, where the Dauphin was crowned on 17 July as Charles VII.

The first known portrayal of Joan of Arc is found in the margin of the Register of the Paris parlement next to an entry that notes her success at Orléans. A later scribe has added a note of her capture at Compiègne on 25 May 1430. (Archives Nationales, Paris)

The Maid sends you news that within eight days, she has chased the English out of every place they held on the river Loire. Many of them are dead or taken prisoner and they have been discomforted in battle … I pray and request that you be ready to come to the anointing of your gracious king Charles at Reims. (Letter of Joan of Arc to the inhabitants of Tournai, 25 June 1429)

Paris was itself under threat. It is fair to say that the Anglo-Burgundians had felt so secure in their conquests that they had made little defensive provision once they had started the advance towards the Loire. The evidence we have of English military activity in 1429–30 shows just how much energy and money had to be expended on the defence of Paris and the Norman frontiers. The garrison establishment was increased from less than 2,000 men to 3,500, and extra companies were installed in the vulnerable places on the eastern frontier.

Paris was saved, largely because Charles lost his nerve and the English poured in over 7,000 troops from England during 1430–31. The English were thus able to prevent further losses. Louviers was recovered after two long sieges, thus returning most of Normandy to English hands. Joan was captured and removed from the scene in May 1431 after her trial at Rouen. The young king Henry VI was then able to travel in some safety to Paris for his coronation in December 1431.

But whilst the early 1430s saw some consolidation, the strains of the years 1429–31 continued to tell, not least in war finances and in the need to maintain defence. It soon became apparent that the English could not hope to extend their territory. Even in Normandy, French incursions began to increase. This most certainly heightened anti-English feeling in the duchy and contributed to the revolt of the peasants of the *pays de Caux* in 1435 and the French penetration of much of Upper Normandy, including the key ports of Dieppe and Harfleur. This forced the English on to the defensive once more, and restricted their war aims to the recovery of the lost areas of the duchy. Shortly before the revolt, the Duke of Burgundy finally declared his true colours and came to treat with Charles VII at Arras. A week earlier, the Duke of Bedford had died at Rouen. 1435 was surely the English *annus horribilis*, and 1436 promised to be no better when Burgundy laid siege to Calais, and Paris fell to Charles.

Again it is perhaps surprising that the English held on and that the war did not end at this point. That it did not is testimony to the massive military effort that the English

The interior of the cathedral at Reims, the traditional crowning place of the kings of France. The fact that Charles VII was crowned here in 1429 was a tremendous fillip to his war against the English. (Anne Curry)

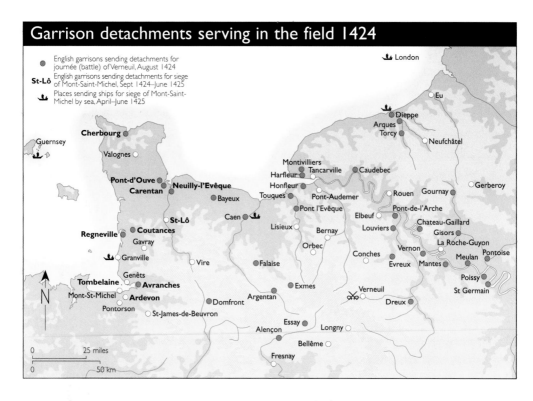

Garrison detachments serving in the field 1424

- English garrisons sending detachments for journée (battle) of Verneuil, August 1424
- **St-Lô** English garrisons sending detachments for siege of Mont-Saint-Michel, Sept 1424–June 1425
- Places sending ships for siege of Mont-Saint-Michel by sea, April–June 1425

London

Eu

Dieppe
Arques
Torcy
Neufchâtel

Guernsey

Cherbourg

Valognes

Montivilliers
Tancarville   Caudebec
Harfleur
Honfleur   Gerberoy
Rouen   Gournay
Pont-d'Ouve
Carentan   Neuilly-l'Evêque   Touques   Pont-Audemer
Bayeux   Pont l'Evêque   Pont-de-l'Arche
Elbeuf   Chateau-Gaillard
St-Lô   Caen   Lisieux   Bernay   Louviers   Gisors
Regneville   Coutances   Orbec   La Roche-Guyon
Gavray   Vernon   Pontoise
Granville   Vire   Conches   Meulan
Evreux   Mantes
Genêts   Falaise
Poissy
Tombelaine   Avranches   Exmes   Verneuil   St Germain
Mont-St-Michel   Ardevon   Argentan   Dreux
Pontorson   Domfront
St-James-de-Beuvron
Essay
Alençon   Longny
Bellême
Fresnay

0   25 miles
0   50 km

N

For sieges and field actions the English relied not only on expeditionary armies from England but also on detachments from the garrisons. The need to face a Franco-Scottish army at Verneuil on 17 August 1424 led to a duchy-wide call out of troops, whereas for the subsequent siege of Mont-Saint-Michel, only places in the near vicinity were asked.

made in 1436, sending a total of around 10,000 troops to the defence of Calais and to Normandy, where the garrison establishment was raised to its highest level of almost 6,000. The English were also helped by Burgundian disinterest and by Charles's caution. This enabled them to recover much of what they had lost in Normandy. Harfleur, an important symbol of English conquest, was recovered in November 1440.

But a defensive position is never easy to maintain. The French held on to Dieppe, placing a garrison of over 1,000 men there at the time of the English siege of 1442. They also held Evreux and Louviers from 1440, forcing a wedge into the English position south of the Seine. Moreover, war damage and economic crisis in Normandy combined to make the *pays de Caux* a depopulated and

unprofitable area. Taxation income fell, whilst defence costs increased. Large numbers of troops from England continued to be needed. Between 1440 and 1443, over 13,000 were sent.

Gascony had been largely devoid of conflict until the late 1430s as both English and French concentrated on the northern lands. The English government's interest in Gascony was renewed in 1439 when there was the possibility of a peace settlement. England now wished to ensure that Gascony's boundaries were as extensive as possible. Thus an expeditionary force of over 2,000 – the largest since 1412 – was sent under the Earl of Huntingdon. Charles VII responded by fortifying the fortresses of the Count of Albret. Initially, Huntingdon's advance met with success, but he was recalled in 1440. In 1442, Charles launched an invasion, taking Dax and St Sever.

The only major surviving feature of the castle at Rouen is the so-called Tour Jeanne d'Arc, although it is uncertain whether Joan was housed here during her trial. (Anne Curry)

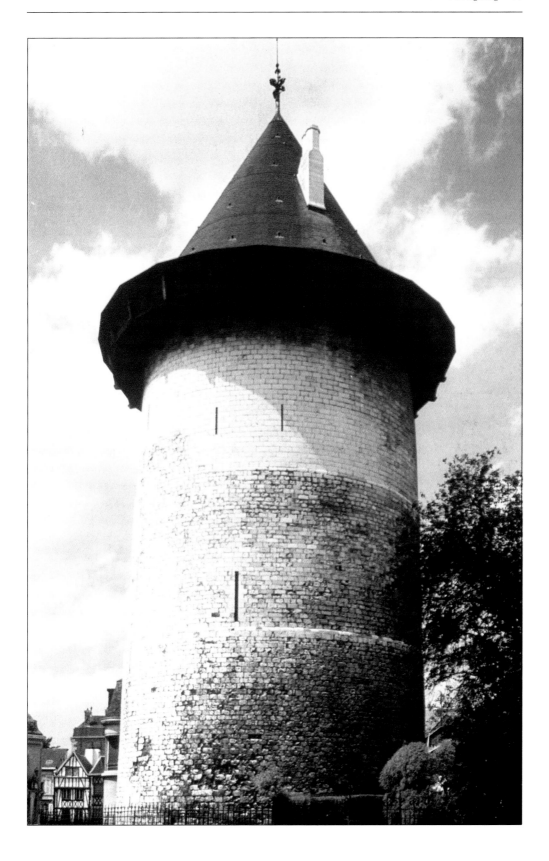

The English responded slowly. Interests in Normandy and in Gascony began to compete for resources. Initially, it was planned that John Beaufort, Earl of Somerset, should cross to Gascony with 800 men-at-arms and 3,400 archers (the increased proportion of archers being clear indication of the financial difficulties in which the English crown found itself), but his charge was subsequently changed to Normandy, and he crossed in 1443 with 800 troops fewer than his indenture had demanded. His strategy of taking the war to the French on the frontiers of Brittany was a complete failure, and had deprived not only Gascony but also Dieppe, to which siege was then being laid, of much needed succour.

This was the last expedition to France. On 28 May 1444, the English agreed a truce with the French, the first cessation of hostilities since 1415. Between these dates, therefore, we have the longest continuous period of conflict of the whole of the Hundred Years' War.

The castle of Dieppe housed an English garrison from its surrender in February 1419. The English felt so secure here that by 1435, only four men-at-arms and 12 archers were stationed there. It is not surprising that the place fell easily to the French in December of that year. (AKG Berlin)

Bertrand du Guesclin; Companions in arms: Andrew Trollope and Osbern Mundeford

Bertrand du Guesclin

Bertrand du Guesclin (c.1320–80) came from a relatively poor cadet branch of the Breton minor nobility, but rose to be France's great hero. Within seven years of his death, a poem on his life was composed by a Picard, Jean de Cuvelier, confirming du Guesclin as a legend in his own time. The poet even tells us that mothers in France, when chastising their children, would say 'be quiet, or else du Guesclin will come to get you'. Richard the Lionheart had been similarly invoked by mothers in the past.

Du Guesclin was short in stature, ugly and careless about his appearance. According to Cuvelier, even when he was a child, his parents despaired of his violence: he was always ready to fight, and organised his peasant friends into rival groups. He ran away to Rennes in his late teens and began to demonstrate his prowess in tournaments, especially that held in June 1337 to celebrate the marriage of Jeanne de Penthièvre and Charles of Blois. Here, with a borrowed horse, he felled 15 other combatants before revealing his identity, to the amazement of the crowd.

In the early stages of the Breton civil war, du Guesclin led a small group of partisans in the region of Rennes in support of Charles's claim to the duchy. In 1350, he took the English-held stronghold of Fougeray by trickery. He waited until the commander had taken most of the garrison to Vannes to assist Thomas Dagworth, and then disguised 30 of his own soldiers as peasants, and even some as women, so that they could enter the place under the guise of delivering timber. These actions were those of a freelance

guerrilla. It was not until the death of his father in 1353, when he inherited the family manor, that he joined the royal army, serving under the marshal of France, Arnoul d'Audrehem, in Lower Normandy.

In 1357, Rennes looked poised to fall to Henry, Duke of Lancaster. Du Guesclin, then in the company of Pierre de Villiers, captain of Pontorson, managed to bring much needed supplies into the city. He followed this with a sortie against the English, who were thereby forced to raise the siege, bringing the French their first piece of good fortune since the capture of King John. Du Guesclin was rewarded by the Dauphin with a grant of 200 livres tournois, hardly a huge sum, but he had come to the notice of the right people.

When de Villiers was called to Paris, du Guesclin took over control of Pontorson, a key garrison on the frontier of Brittany and Normandy, with 120 men under his command. Over the next 23 years he was involved in almost every major theatre, rising through a series of regional commands on behalf of the King and the princes of the blood. He was much relied upon to clear *routiers* from various areas, and for royal actions against Charles of Navarre. Using the age-old tactic of a feigned retreat, he succeeded in defeating the latter at Cocherel on 16 May 1364.

This led to his being created royal chamberlain and Count of Longueville. But he was captured at the battle of Auray on 29 September 1364 when fighting in the cause of Charles of Blois, a reminder that military service for men like du Guesclin was not exclusively for the King. The King assisted in payment of his ransom, and his service thus continued in the later 1360s, leading a 12,000-strong force in support of Henry of Trastamara's ambitions in Castile. Here he was captured again in the Black Prince's victory at Najera on 3 April 1367, by Thomas Cheyne, a man of relatively low rank – a timely reminder that in military action, neither social status nor military

Bertrand du Guesclin's tomb was placed close to that of Charles V in the royal necropolis of Saint-Denis. The effigy may give some idea of the constable's appearance. (Roger-Violett)

reputation rendered combatants less vulnerable. Charles V again assisted in the payment of ransom, which was set by Edward III at 100,000 francs, testimony to du Guesclin's perceived significance.

Du Guesclin served on subsequent campaigns under the King's brother, the Duke of Anjou, against the *routiers* in Languedoc, and under Trastamara in Castile. He was to play a fundamental role in Charles V's battle-avoiding strategy when war reopened in 1369, being appointed constable of France in 1370, and containing the great English *chevauchées* of 1370 and 1373. He also prevented the English seizing Saint-Malo in 1378, although his willingness to negotiate their withdrawal led to criticism at the French royal court. Although du Guesclin had an excellent reputation as a war leader, his relatively low social origin was never forgotten by some. Warfare did offer opportunities for those who could prove their value, yet armies of both sides remained very class based in their structures of command.

Du Guesclin had made it to the top through his own prowess and bravery. At the assault on Charles of Navarre's stronghold of Melun in 1359, for instance, he fought on despite being hit on the head by a large projectile. He was a firm disciplinarian, but he was also much loved by his soldiers because he lived as they did. He was also full of guile and cunning, and was prepared to take risks. Du Guesclin was thus a quintessential soldier who rose from the ranks, not only to be constable, but also to be buried at the order of Charles V next to the King himself in the royal necropolis of Saint-Denis. Cuvelier's poem ends with a poignant death-bed scene where the dying constable calls the marshal to his side.

I entrust to you the care of France. Deliver up to the King of France my sword of tempered steel. Commend me to the King and to all the lords of the land. Pray for me, all of you, for my time has come. Be men of honour. Love each other and serve your crowned king with total loyalty. (Jean Cuvelier, *The Life of the Valiant Bertrand du Guesclin*)

Andrew Trollope and Osbern Mundeford

Trollope came from Thornley, a village in south-east Durham, and was related to cloth dyers. We find him in 1427 as a mounted man-at-arms at the garrison of Fresnay-le-Vicomte on the southern frontier of Normandy, serving under the captaincy of Sir John Fastolf. Amongst his colleagues was Osbern Mundeford of Hockwold in Norfolk, whose father had served on the Agincourt campaign and who was of low-gentry status.

Trollope moved in 1428 to Tombelaine, a particularly uninviting sand-bank location established against French-held Mont-Saint-Michel, but he and Mundeford found themselves together again in Fresnay in the early 1430s. Mundeford was soon specialising in military administration as marshal of the garrison, responsible for discipline and the provision of victuals. Trollope was often deployed in field detachments. In 1433 he was in Fastolf's company reinforcing Caen, and in 1440

served on a raid into Picardy under Matthew Gough, a soldier whose own renown gave him a place in Welsh poetry. Trollope must have distinguished himself with the overall commander, John Beaufort, Earl of Somerset, since he then joined the latter's personal retinue, but by 1442 he was back in Fresnay as lieutenant to the then captain, Sir Richard Woodville.

Mundeford also participated in some field actions in the 1430s, but by 1445 was combining military and civil command as *bailli* and captain of Le Mans and captain of Beaumont-sur-Sarthe. His commander was now Edmund Beaufort, who had succeeded his brother, John, as Earl of Somerset in 1444. Mundeford found himself in a difficult position when asked to implement the royal decision of December 1445 to surrender Maine to the French, but he had to obey orders, even if at first he questioned them. Once Edmund Beaufort had arrived as lieutenant-general of

The English placed a garrison on the rocky outcrop of Tombelaine, close to French-held Mont-Saint-Michel. Andrew Trollope was stationed here in 1428. (Anne Curry)

Normandy in 1448, Mundeford was made treasurer of the duchy, attempting an overhaul of tax collection in 1449. He was also made captain of Pont-l'Evêque and of Fresnay.

In 1449 Trollope was Mundeford's lieutenant at Fresnay. The men were by now brothers-in-law, for Andrew had married Osbern's sister, Elizabeth. Also in the garrison at Fresnay were John Clipsby, a relation on his mother's side, and John Berney, who was his brother-in-law or possibly his stepson, and whose son was given the name Osbern. When Charles VII reopened the war in July, Mundeford was collecting revenues and foodstuffs for English garrisons between Vernon and Mantes, and on 12 August he was amongst those captured at Pont-Audemer. Ten days later he was a prisoner at Chateaudun, where he was interrogated about the fall of Pont-Audemer.

He told us on oath that at 11 or 12 at night he was lying in his bed when he heard a noise in the town and the alarm was raised. He got up but only had time to put on his shirt with his brigandine over the top ... he soon found where the French had broken ten or twelve of the palisades and was able with the help of three or four other English to drive them back ... but two days later, in the middle of the afternoon, he was told that the town was on fire and the French had launched an assault ... as the fire spread, the English took refuge in a stronghold. (Deposition of Mundeford, Bibliothèque Nationale, MS fr. 4054, f. 147).

Trollope as lieutenant surrendered Fresnay to the French in March 1450, but he had not forgotten his companion and brother-in-law: one of the terms of the composition was that Mundeford should be released. The story is made all the more interesting by the fact that both men continued their military careers after the loss of Normandy. In the early 1450s Mundeford was marshal of Calais

and Trollope master porter under Edmund Beaufort as captain.

As the Wars of the Roses escalated, they found themselves 'by the sword divided'. Mundeford was back in England supporting the Lancastrians, but Trollope, still at Calais, was chosen by the Earl of Warwick to take troops to England to assist Richard, Duke of York. Yet old Beaufort loyalties, based on experiences in France, died hard. On the eve of the battle of Ludford Bridge (12 October 1459), Trollope was persuaded to defect to the Lancastrians, plunging the Yorkists into disarray when he disclosed their intended plan of action. He then joined Edmund Beaufort's son, Henry, in an attempt to take Calais from the Yorkists, and was installed as captain of nearby Guînes.

The lives of Mundeford and Trollope were again entwined. In June 1460, Mundeford assembled troops at Sandwich to reinforce Guînes, but Yorkists from Calais fell upon him. Taken across the Channel, he was summarily executed on the sands below the Tour de Rysback. Trollope was forced to surrender Guînes. He made his way back to England where he gained prominence in the Lancastrian victory at Wakefield on 31 December 1460, using subterfuge to entice the Yorkists from their stronghold at Sandal. He also participated in the Lancastrian victory at St Albans (17 February 1461), being knighted after the battle, in which he had been wounded in the foot by a *calletrappe* (a device for damaging horses' hooves).

When the Yorkists seized London, Trollope had a price put on his head. He met his end at the battle of Towton (29 March 1461), sharing command of the Lancastrian vanguard with the Earl of Northumberland. Thus, both Trollope and Mundeford fought and died for their king in France and in England, and, no doubt like many, forged friendships and relationships as they did so.

War cruel and sharp

A war against civilians?

A very important point can be made about the nature of warfare in the Hundred Years' War. Most of it, whether on land or at sea, was conducted within a civilian context. Only battles were restricted to the soldiery. The *chevauchée* was chosen because it was against soft, civilian targets and could have an immediate, demoralising effect. Soldiers on the move ate their way through an area, and took moveable booty as well as burning stored crops and houses. Fortified centres and engagements with enemy troops were generally avoided. It was extremely difficult to respond effectively enough, in that the attackers swiftly moved on to their next target, and communication problems made military intelligence less effective. No one quite knew with *chevauchées* where the attacker would move next. Sieges both involved and affected civilians. Lengthy sieges were particularly harsh on the inhabitants of towns. We are told that the citizens had to eat dogs, cats and even vermin during the six-month siege of Rouen over the winter of 1418–19.

Very little survives of medieval Calais. This sixteenth-century view shows how well defended the town and port was after two centuries of English rule. (British Library)

War was deliberately taken to the people. Such actions against civilians might be deemed legitimate acts of war as they had been licensed by the king. But there were many other acts of destruction and disruption carried out by soldiers of their own volition. Garrison soldiers of both sides often went out 'on their own adventure', and no doubt were given some freedom in deciding from whom booty could be taken, despite disciplinary ordinances for both armies which tried to prevent their attacking civilians. Piracy was encouraged by both the English and French, not least during the period of truce in the late 14th and early 15th centuries.

In France there was also the problem of the lawless bands known as the *routiers*, who continued the war against civilians when they found themselves out of regular military employment. To this we must add the impact of two extremely bitter and violent civil wars, namely between the Dauphin and Charles of Navarre in the late 1350s, which had a particularly marked effect in the Paris Basin, and between the Armagnacs and Burgundians in the early 15th century. Both became enmeshed with the Anglo-French war. At base, it was French war failures that encouraged public disorder and infighting.

Effects on France

It was hard to believe that this was the country I had seen in the past ... I could hardly recognize anything that I had seen before in this kingdom which was once so rich and which was now reduced to ashes. (Petrarch, commenting on the state of France)

There can be little doubt that France was severely damaged physically and economically by the Hundred Years' War. The very title of Henri Deniflé's influential book published between 1897 and 1899, *La désolation des églises, monastères et hopitaux en France pendant la Guerre de cent ans*, epitomises the approach taken and the conclusions drawn, with not even the

church being exempt from attack, especially by the *routiers*. Detailed studies of the Ile-de-France, the Auvergne and Anjou, as well as of major cities such as Toulouse, Tours, Poitiers and Périgueux, have confirmed this view. The values of rents in rural Anjou, for instance, fell by 30–40 per cent over the second half of the 14th century.

A study of Reims is particularly indicative, not least because the city saw a siege by Edward III in 1359 as well as the disturbances of the Navarrese civil war and later English *chevauchées*. Over many decades, peasants flocked into the city for protection, swelling some parishes by 50 per cent. Prices of cereals rocketed: the situation was particularly bad in the late 1350s and 1360s when military actions disrupted the usual trade with towns in the vicinity. The fortification of Reims in the 1350s cost over 100,000 livres tournois, much of it sustained out of local purchase taxes, and involved the demolition of dwellings and religious establishments in the suburbs and in the surrounding area to create a *cordon sanitaire*.

Although there was some recovery in the early 15th century, conditions worsened in the fourth phase of the war. French incursions into Gascony from the early 1440s destroyed vines, which took years of regrowth to recover. In Normandy, the battle for the *pays de Caux* after 1435 led to economic crisis, not least for the ports. The hinterlands of Harfleur and Dieppe were devastated by English armies sent in to recover these places. At Dieppe, the suburb of *Le pollet outre l'eau* (on the other side of the harbour from the main town) was virtually deserted in 1437–38, its residents having 'gone to live elsewhere because of the war'. The English subsequently placed their siege camp there in 1442–43, after which the area was noted as 'completely demolished and ruinous'. It proved impossible to attract the inhabitants back until the English had been driven out of the duchy.

A study of Louviers reveals the damaging effects of recurrent sieges: the town changed hands five times between 1418 and 1440. Revenues from tolls on grain fell from £29 in 1424 to £13 in 1432, with the total value of the town falling from over £191 to £115 over the same period. After the French took the town in 1440 they demolished the cloth hall so that its materials could be used in rebuilding the outer fortifications. Declining rents and agricultural production in the late 1430s and 1440s were so marked that Guy Bois went so far as to term it 'Hiroshima in Normandy', although he admitted that not all economic problems were due to the war. Such circumstances affected not only Normans but also the occupier, for many English had been granted lands in the duchy which were now often of little or no value.

Little now survives of the defences of Harfleur, but this graffito inside the church of St Martin may give some impression, although with artistic licence. (Anne Curry)

Sir John Fastolf, for instance, lost a third of his income of £600 from his French lands as a result of the loss of the *pays de Caux* and the subsequent economic crisis.

The *routiers*

Generally speaking, civilians were in a more protected position when conflict was between royal armies. Even then, the good behaviour of soldiers could not be guaranteed. Indeed, the Jacquerie of 1358 had its immediate cause in a group of the Dauphin's soldiers installing themselves in the fortified abbey of Saint-Leu and ignoring their master's recent order that 'no soldier take, pillage or rob our subjects of corn, wine or any other victuals'.

But the people of France were much more vulnerable when they were exposed to the bands of *routiers*. There can be little doubt that had it not been for the Anglo-French war, the problem of the *routiers* would not have arisen. It had generated a great need for soldiers, more than ever before, but from time to time such men found themselves without paid employment, especially in the aftermath of Brétigny, although the civil war between the Dauphin and Charles of Navarre in the late 1350s had already generated a lawless soldiery prone to waging what was essentially their own war.

Such men were predominantly French but included English and Spanish amongst their number. Interestingly, their organisation often aped that of the formal military structures, in the 'Great Companies' which generated their own war leaders prepared to punish, often savagely, their own men. The raiding practices of the royal armies were tempting to copy – fast-moving, exciting, with easy gains, and a relatively low chance of having to fight against other soldiers. Living off the civilian population was unchallenged at times when central authority was weak. As noted earlier, civilians were a soft target with little in the way of defence, although Wright has emphasised the solidarity generated in their attempts to resist. As he notes, in the Jacquerie the peasants of Saint-Leu were moved by the fact that the Dauphin's order had encouraged them to act against soldiers who misbehaved:

and if soldiers do pillage, we wish and command that anyone may resist them by any method which seems best to them, and to call for help from neighbouring villages by the sound of bells. (Order of March 1357 by the Dauphin Charles)

It was essentially the problem of the *routiers* that led Charles V to restructure his army in the 1360s and 1370s. But it is important to remember that these companies were also from time to time recruited into royal service, not least for activities in Spain in the 1360s and in the invasion of English-held lands after 1369. By the end of the century, employment was also being found further afield, most notably in Italy.

There was a danger of the problem resurfacing in the fourth phase of the war, but not with the same scale or geographical extent as in the previous century. The English had brought in several thousand more soldiers in the mid-1430s, but reduced the garrison establishment again from the early 1440s. This generated the problem of 'men of no retinue or garrison' who were living off the land on the fringes of society. They were a useful pool of manpower on which the English could draw when vacancies arose in garrisons: indeed, their presence explains why such vacancies could be filled very quickly.

The problem of demobilisation was also realised by the French. After the truce of Tours, English and French acted co-operatively in rounding up unemployed soldiers of both sides for a campaign under the Dauphin Louis in Switzerland. Later, the English ordered all of their unemployed soldiers to gather south of Argentan. Some were found garrison posts, those with crafts and lands were ordered to return to them. But all the rest, English, Welsh or Irish, who were found 'not suitable for arms' were marched under guard to Cherbourg and Barfleur in order to be shipped back to England.

Raids on southern England

Raids on England can be compared with the effect of *chevauchées* in France, for they too were conducted against soft civilian targets and were difficult to respond to effectively. By the time the shire levies were called out and dispatched to the coast, the sea-borne raiders, often in oared ships, had moved on to their next target. Sea-borne raids also went for soft targets, with attacks on merchant shipping. The inhabitants of England had not experienced this style of war before, and had little defence against it at the outset of the war.

The raids, or even the threat of them, had a damaging psychological effect. At Friston and East Dean in Sussex, it was reported in 1341 that men did not dare to cultivate their lands 'for fear of the Normans'. A recent study has suggested that it was the rural poor of the south-east who suffered most from the fear and impact of raids, for the wealthy had better defences and enough capital to redeem losses. Indeed, the lack of defence afforded by the crown was certainly a factor in Kentish involvement in the Peasants' Revolt of 1381.

Kent felt the impact of the war in other ways too. The produce of its coastal areas was often reserved for the provisioning of Calais. The latter lay in such an infertile area and often housed such a large garrison – 1,000 or more – that it needed constant resupply from England. This was not popular in the county as it created artificial shortages and higher

The western defences of Southampton, erected over the fronts of existing houses and warehouses in the half-century following the raid of 1338. (Michael Hughes)

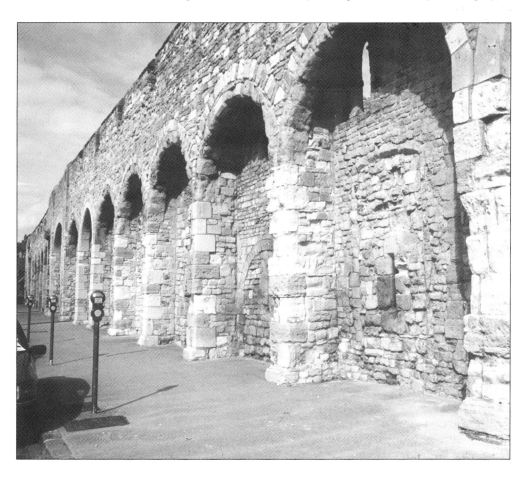

prices. The crown was notoriously slow too in paying for the food it requisitioned for Calais or indeed for anywhere else. There was certainly much complaint early in the war against the king's rights of purveyance – essentially rights of pre-emption, which often resulted in low prices to producers and considerable delays in payments being made. Parliamentary protest led to limitations on the king's rights in the 1350s. Subsequently the crown tended to use contractors to raise its supplies. Generally speaking, the issue was less pronounced in the 15th century when armies could be fed within the occupied territories, but the problem never went away fully.

Kent and Sussex also expressed annoyance in a petition to Parliament in 1429 about the quartering of soldiers, asking that they should not take food without paying for it and that, to improve discipline, soldiers' wages should be distributed before they arrived in the area. It is not surprising, therefore, that the same counties should be amongst those complaining in 1442 about robberies, rape, extortion and violence committed by the soldiery.

The raid on Southampton on 5 October 1338 provides us with a useful case study. At this point, the only defence of the southern and western waterfronts was the gating of streets. (The ability to close off streets was a common policy in French towns too in an effort to keep local order.) There had been no need for defences in the past, and warehouses and houses fronted directly on to the quayside. The raid was carried out on a Sunday when the townspeople were at mass. There can be no doubt of the level of damage caused. The houses of the wealthy in French Street were burned out and lay unoccupied for several years, only being redeveloped towards the end of the century. Over 40 per cent of the properties belonging to the hospital of God's House seem to have been destroyed, leading to a considerable fall in rent income. A licence to appropriate churches granted later to the priory of St Denys noted that even the charters and other muniments held by the priory had

been destroyed by the French. The town seal and weigh beam were certainly carried away, and, of the 194 tuns of red wine in the town, only two tuns remained after the French raiders departed!

No wool was exported from Southampton for a year following the raid, and customs income fell by a half. Likewise at Portsmouth, no customs were collected in the year following its raid of March 1338.

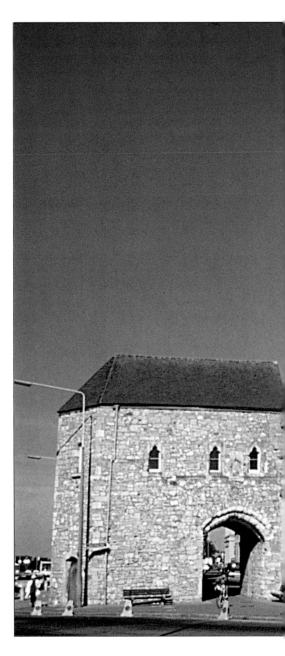

Southampton also suffered long-term decline as Italian merchants transferred their custom to Bristol for the next few years. The town had also been important in the importation of Gascon wine, a trade that more than any other reveals the impact of war.

Clearly there was a need for the fortifications of Southampton to be strengthened, and not least for walls to be built along the southern and western sides of the town. These were finally completed by the end of the century, disrupting the earlier pattern of lanes, buildings and private quays, and blocking off direct access to the waterside. The cost had essentially fallen on

Construction of God's House Tower in the south-east corner of Southampton, intended to control the sluices of the moats and to carry heavy guns, began around 1417. (Michael Hughes)

the inhabitants through the levy of local taxes: in 1376 the townsmen requested the King that he should take the town under his control as they could not support the cost of the defences.

Some interesting developments are seen in the late 14th and 15th centuries as the use of gunpowder artillery increased. The West Gate of Canterbury, which was begun in 1380, is possibly the earliest building constructed with artillery defence in mind. The Catchcold Tower at Southampton was built in the early 1400s with three keyhole gunloops and a vaulted roof to take the weight of cannon. God's House Tower dates from slightly later. In the face of invasion threats in 1386, Thomas Tredington, chaplain, was installed in the castle at Southampton, not only to celebrate the divine service but also to keep the artillery because of his expertise in this area. By 1449–50, the town's gunner, 'Harry Gunner', was kept busy making chambers for the breech-loading guns common in this period,

as well as in buying gunstones, and 'two bags of leather for putting the gunpowder in'.

War and English trade

War, trade and international relations were highly interdependent. Communications between England and its continental holdings were completely dependent on the sea route. As Gascony was not a very fertile area, it imported much of its grain, as well as other commodities such as wool and cloth, from England. In return, it was England's main source of sweet wine, and salt also came into England from the Bay of Biscay. Friendly relations with Brittany were thus vital in ensuring the security of the route, and Breton pirates were a major problem when relations with the duchy were hostile. Flanders was England's major trading partner, but technically part of France. It is no coincidence that Edward III began his attack on Philip VI by

A breech-loading handgun from the mid-15th century now in the Musée des Beaux Arts at Rouen. These guns were easy to manufacture but prone to backfire or to break as the shot was issued. (Anne Curry)

the second. Raids on England were much assisted by the galleys provided as a result.

There was undoubtedly an effect on trade. A graph of the quantities of wine shipped to England, on which the crown took custom, shows a major downturn at the opening of the war. In 1335–36, 74,000 tuns had been exported from Bordeaux. The figure fell to 16,500 tuns in the following year, and to 6,000 tuns in 1348–49. The trade never fully recovered.

Another cause of economic loss for traders was the crown's right to impress merchant ships and crews. The English crown never had a large navy of its own and was dependent on impressment to provide not only transports but also warships. This cut into trading activities. Norfolk fishermen particularly resented being called out at the height of the herring season. Great Yarmouth's decline in the post-Black Death period has been traced to the disruption of shipping as a result of the war. Given the location of Edward III's early campaigns, it was frequently called upon to supply vessels: between 1335 and 1340 half of its merchant fleet was customarily in royal service. English wool export also certainly declined, but there was some compensation in the stimulus to domestic cloth production for export.

manipulating the wool supply in order to force alliances from the Brabanters and Flemish, nor that the Flemish cloth towns of Bruges, Ypres and Ghent, so dependent upon English wool, should pursue different policies from their count. For the English, Calais became a staple port through which exports had to pass.

Later, the tenure of Flanders and an increasingly large part of the Low Countries by the dukes of Burgundy further complicated Anglo-French relations. The Anglo-Burgundian alliance was central to the success of the English in the third phase of the war, and even in the fourth phase when the Duke defected to Charles VII, truces were agreed to allow commercial links between England and the Low Countries to continue, a reminder that wars in this period did not necessarily lead to the complete severance of trade. The French had important alliances too, not least those that brought them naval and military support – the Genoese in the first phase of the war, and the Castilians in

War and taxation in England and France

In England, the consent of the Commons in Parliament was needed for the grant of the lay subsidy. This brought the war fully within the public gaze. Whilst Parliament could not in practice refuse grants, it might impose conditions, such as the appointment of war treasurers at times when it felt that some of the taxes were being diverted to domestic purposes or into the pockets of certain officials. In 1376 and 1386, impeachments of ministers occurred where charges included peculation and the mishandling of funds for the war. The English were doing particularly badly at this stage. Efforts to raise more revenues through new taxes – the poll taxes levied on everyone over a certain age – led to the Peasants' Revolt of 1381.

Thenceforward, the English crown had to make do with its lay subsidy, which it was forced to reduce for some places in the wake of economic decline in the 1430s and 1440s. Thus the previous income of around £38,000 fell to around £30,000, with the income of taxation from the clergy showing a similar fall from £20,000 in the 14th century to £10,000–17,000 in the 15th. As Ormrod has shown, revenue from customs duties fell from the 1360s onwards. Thus there can be no doubt that the kings of England were in a weaker financial position in the 15th century than they had been earlier. That they achieved so much after 1415 was due to their conquest of territory in France that enabled them to levy taxation there. When their territorial control diminished in the fourth phase of the war, they found themselves in considerable financial difficulties and unable to raise enough revenue on either side of the Channel.

In France, the Hundred Years' War led to a considerable extension of the taxing powers of the crown. At the outset, tax was essentially an occasional payment in lieu of military service when the *arrière-ban* was called. From 1341 royal income was increased by virtue of the salt tax (*gabelle*), but Henneman's study of finances shows how precarious the French position remained, not least in the wake of the defeats of 1346 and 1356 when there was no choice but to call the Estates. John's ransom also prompted the levy of more hearth taxes (*fouages*) and purchase taxes (*aides* and *quatrièmes*), and was a major burden for all.

Reims was forced to contribute 20,000 écus despite its fragile economic state in the wake of the military action of 1359, and had to borrow from Italian financiers. These loans were still being repaid when the city had a further burden on it for the coronation of Charles V in 1364, to the tune of over 77,000 livres tournois.

On his deathbed Charles V abolished the *fouage*, 'wishing to relieve the people to some degree of the taxes imposed upon them', and his son's government was soon forced to abolish the *aides* and *gabelle* too. Initial attempts to reimpose them led to popular rebellion in 1382, but the failure of the rebellion, very much connected to the victory over the Flemish rebel militias at Roosebeke in 1382, led to their re-introduction. Two years later, direct *tailles*, like the English lay subsidy, began to be imposed. In order to win support in the civil war, John the Fearless, Duke of Burgundy, abolished the *aides* in 1418: the Dauphin had little choice but to do the same in his area of control. But the demands of war forced their renewal again. By 1439, taxation was in practice permanent in the France ruled by Charles VII, and was instrumental in his setting up of what was in effect a standing army in the companies of the *ordonnance* and *francs archers*.

The French crown had the greatest potential to increase its tax revenues. Despite several false starts it succeeded in increasing its revenue during the war. Thus, whereas English royal tax income diminished over the course of the Hundred Years' War, French revenues from the same source increased, about 45,000 livres tournois being raised in 1338, rising to 70,000 in the 1340s, and 155,000 by 1460. There was a further phenomenal rise under Louis XI, especially through the *taille*, so that his revenue in 1483 was at 450,000 livres tournois.

Christine de Pizan

Christine was born in Venice around 1365, but came to France in the late 1360s when her father took up office as astrologer and physician at the court of Charles V. In 1379, she married a Picard nobleman, Etienne de Castel, one of the King's secretaries and notaries, but by the late 1380s she had lost both father and husband, and found herself with two young children and little income. She had been well educated by her father, and continued to read avidly. At first, she made money by copying manuscripts but

Christine de Pizan is here portrayed, clad in the distinctive garb of a widow, presenting her work, the *Epitre d'Othée*, to Charles VI around 1400. (Bodleian Library, Oxford)

then began to compose her own works, which together make her one of the most famous and respected authors of the Middle Ages. Her output was prolific in poetry and prose, and covers a wider range of themes. For our purposes, she is of interest because she lived through three phases of the war and produced writings reflecting her experience of them. Furthermore, she was living in Paris at the very heart of affairs, and certainly had personal knowledge of many of the principal actors in the war.

The second phase of the war is represented in her life of Charles V, which she was commissioned to write by one of his sons, Philip the Bold, Duke of Burgundy, in 1404. The tone of this work is well reflected in its title, *Le Livre des faits et bonnes moeurs du roi Charles V le sage* (*The Book of the Deeds and Good Habits of King Charles the Wise*). In the military context, Christine singles out for praise his reorganisation of the army, so that each company was under its own leader. His preparedness for war after he had sent his defiance to the English is also praised. He was careful in ensuring the prompt payment of his troops. Although he was obliged to raise large armies, he levied the resultant taxes 'without oppression'. 'Our king was a chivalrous sovereign ... the defender and faithful guardian of all.' But Christine also stresses his wisdom in avoiding battle.

But fearing reversal of Fortune, he judged wisely that it was not healthy for the Prince to put himself into battle save in dire necessity. For the whole body and its limbs will be weakened if the head is damaged. The capture or death of the king leads to the effective death of all his subjects. (Christine de Pizan, *The Book of the Deeds and Good Habits of King Charles the Wise*)

Christine's works also reflect the destructive impact that the civil war between the Burgundians and the Armagnacs had on French society. This is particularly noticeable in the letter that she addressed to Queen Isabeau, the wife of Charles VI, in 1405. At this point, the Duke of Orléans was assembling his men against the Duke of Burgundy in Paris. Christine urged Isabeau to 'heal the sickness and division in the kingdom' by acting as mediator, a role often assigned to royal and noble women in this period. There was little doubt in Christine's mind that 'the kingdom will be destroyed if it is divided amongst itself', as it certainly was at this point, with 'the heirs and children of the noble blood of France pillaging the kingdom'.

The third phase of the war was an even more demoralising experience for the French. The defeat at Agincourt prompted Christine to write a work of spiritual consolation, *L'Epistre de la prison de la vie humaine* (*The Letter of the Prison of Human Life*) (1416–18), for Marie de Berry, daughter of the Duke. It does not mention the battle by name. (Rather like actors who wish to avoid bad luck by speaking of the 'Scottish play' instead of *Macbeth*, so the French spoke of 'the accursed day' rather than saying 'Agincourt'.) But it is clear from the text that this event was the stimulus, as it had brought so much sorrow to the 'ladies of honour' of France through the deaths and captivities of their loved ones. Marie had lost her son-in-law, the Count of Nevers, in the battle and had had her husband, Jean de Bourbon, and her son, the Count of Eu, captured.

In the summer of 1418, as the English advanced in their conquest of Normandy, and the Burgundians entered Paris, Christine, a supporter of the Armagnac faction, took refuge in the nunnery at Poissy, where her daughter was already a nun. Her son John went south with the Dauphin and died in exile. But Christine lived to see the tide turn.

In 1429 the sun began to shine again ... the reason is that the rejected child of the rightful king of France, who has suffered many a great misfortune ... has risen up, coming as a crowned king in might and majesty, wearing spurs of gold. (Christine de Pizan, *Ditié de Jeanne d'Arc*)

She celebrated Joan of Arc's raising of the siege of Orléans and the subsequent crowning of Charles VII with her last known work, *Ditié de Jeanne d'Arc* (*The Tale of Joan of Arc*), written only two weeks after the coronation. This also provides us with the earliest panegyric on Joan, who had saved the kingdom – 'something 5,000 men could not have done' – although, to be fair, Christine does give some praise to 'you trusty men-at-arms who carried out the task and proved yourselves to be good and loyal'. Christine compares Joan with Old Testament heroines and predicts that she will lead Charles to the ultimate victory, the reconquest of the Holy Land.

Christine displays throughout her writings a keen interest in the war, but nowhere more so than in her *Livre des fais d'armes et de chevalerie* (*Book of the Feats of Arms and Chivalry*), written in 1410 probably under commission from John the Fearless, Duke of Burgundy. It was completely unprecedented that a woman should write a military treatise. Although the work is dependent upon Honoré de Bonet's military treatise of 1386, the *Tree of Battles*, and on the fourth-century treatise of Vegetius, *De re militari*, which was the main military manual throughout the whole of the Middle Ages, Christine does add her own perspective. For instance, she recalls the battle of Roosebeke in 1382 when the French defeated the Flemish townsmen. She also gives much detail on the provisions and equipment needed for the defence of strongholds. All in all this is an intriguing work by an equally intriguing writer, and one that found its way to an English audience through Caxton's translation and printing of 1489.

Charles VII as portrayed by Fouquet. Once he had been crowned king, Joan of Arc's role became less significant, despite Christine de Pizan's hopes expressed in the *Ditié de Jeanne d'Arc*. (Louvre)

Let us consider 200 men-at-arms with their servants, two each, to be fed for six months. You would need 110 measures of wheat according to the Parisian measure, a third of which should be in the form of bread and the rest as flour ... twelve cannons throwing stones, two of which will be larger than the others in order to break up the machines, mantelets and other coverings ... 3,000 pounds of lead to make shot for the cannons, six dozen iron-tipped lances ... eight bellows for countermining ... six dozen wooden shovels ... (Christine de Pizan, *Book of the Feats of Arms and Chivalry*, part 2, chapter 16)

The loss of Normandy and Gascony

The end of the Hundred Years' War came with the loss of Normandy in 1449–50, followed by that of Gascony in 1453. These events reflect the success of recent French military reforms, whilst also demonstrating the political and military disarray in which the English had put themselves after the truce of Tours of May 1444.

If the English intended to use the truce to fortify their position, as the Duke of Suffolk implied to the parliament of 1445, then they went a strange way about it. They undertook defence cuts to save money, since, in time of truce, they could not ask for heavy taxation from the Norman Estates. The garrisons in Normandy were reduced from about 3,500 to 2,500 men in June 1444, and may have fallen to 2,000 by 1448. Inadequate attention was paid to the maintenance of fortifications and to the provision of artillery. Castles and towns were thus easy pickings for Charles VII after he declared war on 17 July 1449. By reducing the garrisons, the English had lost the capacity to send detachments into the field. The expeditionary forces dispatched from England in 1450 were too little, too late.

The French, on the other hand, capitalised on the truce. Building on the arrangements made by Charles V, the King created more companies of cavalry to produce 12,000 men. Each company contained 100 'lances', each containing a man-at-arms, a *coutiller* ('knife man'), a page, two archers (still crossbow-men), and a *valet de guerre*. To these he added, by means of an order issued in 1448, the obligation that each parish should provide one archer, producing a total of 8,000 *francs archers*. Together these constituted an army on permanent standby, although only paid when in active service, and still supplemented by troops raised through the *semonce des nobles* and *arrière-ban*. A strong

artillery train was also developed under the direction of the Bureau brothers. Charles had also gained the important military alliance of Duke Francis of Brittany.

We have now taken steps to ensure the safety of our kingdom in case the truce between us and our nephew of England does not bring peace. For it is right and proper that we should establish in our kingdom a number of men for its defence whom we can use in our service in time of war without having to employ those who are not our subjects … in each parish there shall be one archer who will keep himself always ready and equipped for war with a sallet, dagger, sword, bow, sheath of arrows, jerkin and a short coat of mail. (Order of Charles VII, 28 April 1448)

Charles cannot have been unaware of the weakness of the English defences. Henry VI had already shown himself vulnerable to pressure, for in December 1445 he had agreed to surrender Maine. Although this was intended to assist in peace negotiations, it was a foolish decision because it weakened his diplomatic position and undermined morale. English soldiers such as Osbern Mundeford could not believe that their king and commanders had agreed to it, but they had little choice but to withdraw from Maine in March 1448. The sight of demobilised soldiers and settlers drifting through Normandy can hardly have boosted the confidence of those in the garrisons of the duchy, whose own pay was increasingly erratic now that the tax income was reduced, but who found their freedom of action and opportunities for booty limited by the need to observe the truce.

Under such circumstances, it seems even greater folly that the English should give the French an excuse to break the truce by

The defeat of the English 1429–50

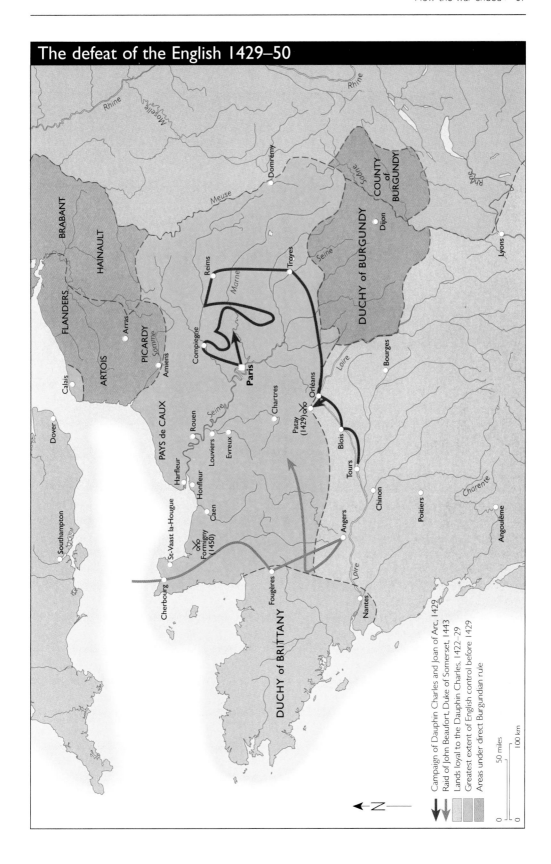

Campaign of Dauphin Charles and Joan of Arc, 1429
Raid of John Beaufort, Duke of Somerset, 1443
Lands loyal to the Dauphin Charles, 1422–29
Greatest extent of English control before 1429
Areas under direct Burgundian rule

BRABANT
HAINAULT
FLANDERS
Arras
PICARDY
Somme
Amiens
ARTOIS
Calais
PAYS de CAUX
Dover
Rouen
Louviers
Evreux
Harfleur
Honfleur
Caen
Southampton
St-Vaast la-Hougue
Cherbourg
Formigny
(1450)
DUCHY of BRITTANY
Fougères
Nantes
Angers
Chinon
Tours
Poitiers
Angoulême
Charente
Loire
Blois
Patay
(1429)
Orléans
Bourges
Loire
Chartres
Paris
Compiègne
Reims
Marne
Troyes
Seine
Seine
Meuse
Domrémy
Rhine
Moselle
Rhine
DUCHY of BURGUNDY
Dijon
COUNTY
of
BURGUNDY
Saône
Lyons

N

0   50 miles
0   100 km

The castle of Fougères in Brittany, just across the frontier of Normandy, which was seized by François de Surienne in March 1449, leading to the reopening of the Anglo-French war after almost five years of truce. (Anne Curry)

capturing Fougères on 24 March 1449. This fortress lay within Brittany. Thus the attack on it served to bring the Duke closer to support of Charles VII. The English had hoped to do the opposite: their plan had been to put pressure on Duke Francis to release from captivity his pro-English brother, Giles.

The assault on Fougères was a gamble. War leaders tried to argue that it was an independent action carried out by an Arragonese mercenary who had long been in their pay, Sir François l'Arragonais. (L'Arragonais is himself a fascinating example of the kind of soldier the war produced – holder of the Garter, but later master of the Duke of Burgundy's artillery and the recipient of a pension from Louis XI.) Research has shown that the plan was officially endorsed: the garrisons of Lower Normandy had been reinforced shortly before, with a campaign in Brittany perhaps intended. The taking of Fougères might have

assisted the English military and diplomatic position had it been followed up by further action, but instead l'Arragonais found himself without aid and was forced to evacuate the place.

The truce had already shown itself a fragile beast, being renewed only for short periods, with many disputes over supposed infractions. It is clear that Charles was keen for an opportunity to attack (his readiness for invasion and his diplomatic dealings with Brittany give sound proof of this), but as the English were so obviously unprepared, it was suicidal that they should give him the excuse he needed.

In Normandy there was a change of leadership. The lieutenant-general, Richard, Duke of York, had been recalled at the end of 1445. A year later, Edmund Beaufort, Duke of Somerset, replaced him, but he did not cross until May 1448. He was certainly not lacking in experience or ability, and tried hard to improve military discipline and to deal with the complaints of inhabitants. He was fully aware of the vulnerability of the duchy, as his letter read in Parliament in the spring of 1449 makes clear.

If war should occur, which God forbid, Normandy is no way sufficient in itself to offer resistance against the great might of the enemy. For there is no place in the King's obedience provided for in terms of repairs, ordnance, or any kind of artillery … almost all places have fallen into such ruin that even were they to be stocked up with men and ordnance, they could not be defended. (Roll of Parliament)

Somerset also said that the Estates of Normandy could bear no more taxation. But Parliament was reluctant to vote English money. Its suggestion that those English granted lands in the duchy should donate part of their revenues was a good example of how little those at home knew of the realities of the situation: many settlers had lost their lands after 1435 or else seen incomes diminished by war and by an economic downturn. The situation was not assisted by the King's lack of enthusiasm, or by growing political machinations, which encouraged many leading captains to stay in England.

The loss of the duchy further exacerbated political problems at home. A scapegoat had to be found. Suffolk thus found himself impeached early in 1450 whilst the towns and castles of the duchy continued to fall. Sentenced to exile, he was lynched on his way out of England. Popular disquiet that the duchy fell so easily and without the English government offering resistance is also demonstrated by Cade's rebellion in May–June 1450. Amongst other things, the rebels urged that the 'traitors' responsible should be brought to book. In the years that followed, York, who had himself lost much land in Normandy, stressed the culpability of Somerset. This was in effect the origin of the dispute that culminated in the first battle of the Wars of the Roses at St Albans in 1455, where Somerset met his death.

The loss of Normandy was swift and largely unchallenged. Places had already started to fall even before the declaration of war. Pont-de-l'Arche, an important defence for Rouen, was captured on 16 May 1449 with the aid of a merchant of Louviers. The willingness of the inhabitants of Normandy to betray their towns to the French king is revealed on many subsequent occasions over the next year, reminding us that military outcomes were as dependent upon local opinion as on the effectiveness of troops. It is easy to say that the Normans had simply been waiting for liberation from the foreign occupier, and that they had only been kept in check by English military presence, but the issue of loyalty was much more complex and varied, and much affected by the desire of civilians to preserve their own livelihoods. For them, the power worthy of support was the one that could maintain the peace. Before 1449 this had been the English, now it was the French.

Normandy was invaded from the north-east by the Counts of Saint-Pol and Eu, from the east along the Seine by the Count of Dunois and Duke of Alençon and later the King along the Seine, and from the south-west by the Duke of Brittany and his uncle, Arthur de Richemont, a veteran of Agincourt. Literally, they swept everything before them in a *blitzkrieg*. Scarcely anywhere held out for longer than a few days. Once Rouen surrendered on 29 October at the behest of its inhabitants, the English cause was irredeemable. Charles 'le très victorieux' (the most victorious) was welcomed into the Norman capital and elsewhere in triumph.

By January 1450, only Caen, Bayeux, Falaise and the Cotentin remained in English hands. Here a brief revival occurred when English reinforcements under Sir Thomas Kyriell arrived at Cherbourg, but a decisive blow was dealt at the battle of Formigny on 15 April, where the English were emphatically defeated. This battle is significant because its outcome depended on the Count of Clermont's judicious use of gunfire to draw the larger English army out of its defensive position. The potential power of the artillery train built up by Charles had already been apparent at the capture of Mantes, but there the inhabitants had decided to surrender to avoid destruction of the walls on which they had lavished much taxation. After Formigny, the French moved inexorably up the Cotentin. On 12 August, the last English-held place, Cherbourg, surrendered.

The battlefield of Formigny, to the west of Bayeux, where the English were defeated on 15 April 1450. Their removal from Norman soil was now only a matter of time. (Anne Curry)

Charles now turned his attention to Gascony with an army of 7,000, many of whom had served in Normandy, knowing that he had already received offers of support from nobility in the duchy. Bordeaux surrendered to Dunois on 30 June 1451. The English raised an army of 3,000 under Sir Richard Woodville, a veteran of the Norman campaigns, but the dispatch of the force was postponed from its original date of 18 October 1450, and it is unlikely that any troops reached the duchy. By August it had been cancelled because of fears of a French invasion of south-west England and the need to send reinforcements to Calais.

In the following year there were competing interests: Calais and the Channel Islands; an armed fleet at sea; and relief to Gascony. An army of 5,000 was raised under Talbot for the sea, but then sent to Gascony, where it recaptured Bordeaux on 20 October 1452 with the aid of partisans. The French had expected Talbot to land in Normandy. Many of the cavalry companies were still stationed there, and the *francs archers* had also been summoned to the coast. Gascony had thus been left relatively undefended.

A relief force of 2,000 was sent from England in the spring of 1453, but another due in August never crossed. Charles was able to deploy a force of 8,000. Talbot was defeated and killed at the battle of Castillon on 17 July. Here he used the customary tactic of an attack on foot. But on this occasion it was the English who were mown down by French arrow fire, and also by gunshot. Bordeaux held out for a further three months, but without the possibility of aid from England the city had to surrender on 19 October 1453. The English now had only Calais.

A defining moment in history?

We might expect a war to end with some kind of peace settlement that reflected and reinforced the victory of one side over the other. There was no negotiated settlement for the end of the Hundred Years' War. Calais remained in English hands until 1558, and it was not until the Treaty of Amiens of 1801 that the title 'king of France' was abandoned: by then, of course, France no longer had a monarch.

A recurrent theme in the history of Europe between the late-15th century and the mid-19th century was Anglo-French hostility. But 1453 has much to recommend it as both the end of an era and the end of a war. It marked the final loss of the lands in south-west France which had been held by English kings since the 12th century. If we accept that these lands were the *real* long-term cause of Anglo-French hostilities, then their loss was a major turning point in Anglo-French relations. Never again were the English able to support a meaningful claim to the French throne by virtue of a major presence in France.

The fact that Normandy had been lost only a few years earlier was most significant. The occupation of Normandy had given the English control of one of the wealthiest and most strategically significant areas of France. And it had been lost all too easily. Worse still, it proved impossible to effect any recovery of any of the lost lands. Resources had to be poured into the defence of Calais. Henry VI's descent into madness in the summer of 1453, which created governmental paralysis and further fanned divisions, not least between Somerset and York, towards civil war, was no doubt a major factor in why no effort was made to invade France again after 1453, although a shortage of money was also influential. The enormity of the task was self-evident, not least because Charles VII, at

first worried that the English would return, had ensured the firm defence of his conquests, and had encouraged attacks on the English coasts and shipping.

French historians have made it quite clear that Charles's authority was much boosted by the recovery of Normandy and Gascony. So emphatic were the victories that he chose to exploit them for propaganda purposes and his loyal people followed in his wake. Economic recovery was slow but was assisted by the fact that the recoveries had been easy and not physically destructive.

With the heart of a lion and courage of a prince he entered Normandy with a large army and by sieges, battles and surprise attacks as well as other means he drove you English out in one season, which is a very short time indeed. He has left you not a single place ... conquering all that you and your king Henry had conquered in thirty-three years. (Treatise known as *The Debate of the Heralds of England and France*, c.1455)

All in all, therefore, the French emerged stronger from the war and the English weaker. Even though both suffered civil war in the decades that followed, it was in England that royal authority was dealt a major blow in the Wars of the Roses, whereas both Charles VII and his son, Louis XI, began the road to absolutism. Their military reforms and increased use of gunpowder artillery, backed up by a further expansion in royal authority and taxing capacity, paved the way for the large armies of the early modern period and in particular for French intervention in Italy at the turn of the century. In England, the armies imploded on themselves. Many who served Lancaster and York in the Wars of the Roses had been in the English army in France. We saw two examples earlier in Trollope and Mundeford.

From the historian's privileged position of hindsight, there can be no doubt that the end of the Hundred Years' War, and indeed the whole war itself, were defining moments in English and French history. The war had been by far the most long-standing, and the most militarily and politically significant, conflict in western Europe in the later Middle Ages. It had involved virtually every other state at one time or another. It had divided France twice, in 1360 and in 1420 – events that did much to embitter the French towards the English. Their very freedom and existence were under threat.

The claim to the French throne was perhaps at the forefront of English ambitions only from the assassination of John the Fearless in 1419, but its very use since 1340 had elevated the war to a new status – no longer a war between vassal and sovereign but between two sovereigns. In such a scenario it is not surprising that ideas of national identity hardened and insults were traded between the two nations. They remained 'wars of kings' throughout, but the nature of the fighting, which targeted civilians in a way that they were powerless to resist, and the level of the taxation burden made them also 'wars of peoples'. The expression 'society at war' does indeed seem appropriate.

There can be no doubt of the war's importance in military terms. Because of its length and intensity, and the fact that it was often waged in several areas simultaneously, it had prompted an increase in the number of men for whom soldiering was a primary occupation. It had persuaded the English and French to increase the proportion of archers in their armies in order to generate numerical presence and effective 'human mass artillery'. It had increased demands for weapons, armour and fortifications, and had no doubt encouraged the development of gunpowder artillery. In this, the English had not moved as quickly as the French, being too complacent in their defence of Normandy and Gascony, and being constrained by the difficulties of holding lands overseas. But it had generated in Normandy what was essentially an English standing army, which was then outmatched by Charles VII's military advances of the mid-1440s.

The Hundred Years' War saw many forms of warfare, but a final note can be sounded about its major battles. It has become fashionable to downplay the significance of battles and to bring to mind that they were the least common form of conflict. None of the battles of the war was decisive – no form of medieval warfare could be decisive, as the scale was too small and the impact too localised. But Sluys, Crécy, Poitiers, La Rochelle, Agincourt, Patay and Formigny all had marked catalytic effects on the course of the conflict in a way that no other forms of action did or could have done. For contemporaries these were the defining moments, and clear testimony of the seriousness and bitterness with which the Hundred Years' War was fought.

The battlefield of Agincourt. The road between the villages of Tramecourt and Agincourt probably passes through the heart of the battle. The clump of trees is the site of a grave pit. (Anne Curry)

Further reading

Allmand, C. T., *The Hundred Years War: England and France at War c.1300–c.1450*, 1988.

Allmand, C. T., *Lancastrian Normandy: The History of a Medieval Occupation 1415–1450*, 1983.

Allmand, C. T., *Society at War: The Experience of England and France during the Hundred Years War*, new edition, 1998.

Ayton, A., *Knights and Warhorses: Military Service and the English Aristocracy under Edward III*, 1994.

Barber, R., *Life and Campaigns of the Black Prince*, 1979.

Barnie, J., *War in Medieval Society: Social Values and the Hundred Years War 1337–1399*, 1974.

Bennett, M., *Agincourt 1415*, 1991.

Contamine, P., *War in the Middle Ages*, English edition trans. M. Jones, 1984.

Curry, A., ed., *Agincourt 1415: Henry V, Sir Thomas Erpingham and the Triumph of the English Archers*, 2000.

Curry, A., *The Battle of Agincourt: Sources and Interpretations*, 2000.

Curry, A., *The Hundred Years War*, 1993.

Curry, A. and Hughes, M., eds, *Arms, Armies and Fortifications in the Hundred Years War*, 1994.

DeVries, K., *Medieval Military Technology*, 1992

DeVries, K., *Infantry Warfare in the Early Fourteenth Century*, 1996.

Fowler, K., *The Age of Plantagenet and Valois*, 1967.

Fowler, K., *Medieval Mercenaries*, Vol. 1: *The Great Companies*, 2001.

Friel, I., *The Good Ship: Ships, Shipbuilding and Technology in England 1200–1520*, 1995.

Froissart, Jean, *Chronicles*, ed. G. Brereton, 1968.

Green, D., *The Black Prince*, 2001.

James, T. B. and Simons, J. (eds), *The Poems of Laurence Minot*, 1989.

Jones, M., *Ducal Brittany 1364–1399*, 1970.

Jones, M. and Vale, M. G. A., eds, *England and her Neighbours in the Middle Ages*, 1989.

Keen, M., *The Laws of War in the Late Middle Ages*, 1965.

Keen, M., ed., *Medieval Warfare: A History*, 1999.

Lewis, P., *Later Medieval France: The Polity*, 1968.

Lucas, H. S., *The Low Countries and the Hundred Years War*, 1929.

Nicolle, D., *Medieval Warfare Sources Book*, Vol. 1: *Warfare in Western Christendom*, 1995.

Palmer, J. J. N., *England, France and Christendom, 1377–1399*, 1972.

Pernoud, R. and Clin, Marie-Veronique, *Joan of Arc: Her Story*, 2000.

Perroy, E., *The Hundred Years War*, 1951.

Pollard, A. J., *John Talbot and the War in France 1426–1453*, 1983.

Prestwich, M., *Armies and Warfare in the Middle Ages: The English Experience*, 1996.

Rogers, C. J., *War Cruel and Sharp: English Strategy under Edward III, 1327–1360*, 2000.

Rogers, C. J., ed., *The Wars of Edward III*, 2000.

Sumption, J., *The Hundred Years War*, Vol. 1: *Trial by Battle*, 1990.

Sumption, J., *The Hundred Years War*, Vol. 2: *Trial by Fire*, 1999.

Vale, M. G. A., *English Gascony 1399–1413*, 1970.

Vale, M. G. A., *The Angevin Legacy and the Hundred Years War 1250–1340*, 1990, republished as *The Origins of the Hundred Years War*, 1996.

Vale, M. G. A., *War and Chivalry: Warfare and Aristocratic Culture in England, France and Burgundy at the End of the Middle Ages*, 1981.

Willard, C., ed., *The Book of Deeds of Arms and of Chivalry, by Christine de Pizan*, 1999.

Wright, N., *Knights and Peasants: The Hundred Years War in the French Countryside*, 1998.

Index

Related titles & companion series from Osprey

CAMPAIGN (CAM)

**Strategies, tactics and battle experiences
of opposing armies**

WARRIOR (WAR)

**Motivation, training, combat experiences
and equipment of individual soldiers**

ELITE (ELI)

**Uniforms, equipment, tactics and personalities
of troops and commanders**

NEW VANGUARD (NVG)

**Design, development and operation
of the machinery of war**

MEN-AT-ARMS (MAA)

**Uniforms, equipment, history
and organisation of troops**

ORDER OF BATTLE (OOB)

**Unit-by-unit troop movements and
command strategies of major battles**

Contact us for more details – see below

ESSENTIAL HISTORIES (ESS)

**Concise overviews of major wars
and theatres of war**

To order any of these titles, or for more information on Osprey Publishing, contact:

Osprey Direct (UK) Tel: +44 (0)1933 443863 Fax: +44 (0)1933 443849 E-mail: info@ospreydirect.co.uk

Osprey Direct (USA) c/o MBI Publishing Toll-free: 1 800 826 6600 Phone: 1 715 294 3345

Fax: 1 715 294 4448 E-mail: info@ospreydirectusa.com

www.ospreypublishing.com